"Revival *is a gracious gift that we will all benefit from reading. The commentary is written from the personal perspective of a superb preacher who has a pastor's heart and knows how to make the past come alive in order to strengthen our own experiences. Prepare to be transformed."*

–Richard P. Heitzenrater, William Kellon Quick Professor Emeritus of Church History and Wesley Studies at Duke Divinity School; author of *Wesley and the People Called Methodists* and editor of *The Works of John Wesley: Bicentennial Edition*

"Adam Hamilton connects John Wesley's contribution in 18th-century England with his legacy for 21st-century America, bringing lessons from Wesley's life and ministry to bear on discipleship today. This is an excellent resource for personal and denominational revival."

–Scott J. Jones, Resident Bishop of the Great Plains area of The United Methodist Church; author of *Wesley and the Quadrilateral* and *The Wesleyan Way.*

"Hamilton takes us on a pilgrimage to the places where the Methodist revival began, and it quickly becomes a journey into the heart and soul of what it means to follow Christ in the Wesleyan tradition. The book is both informative and inspirational and can make a vital contribution to reenergizing the Methodist movement in our time."

–James A. Harnish, author of *A Disciple's Path* and *Simple Rules for Money*

"Hamilton possesses an extraordinary gift for describing complicated events, relationships, and concepts simply and profoundly. In this work, he breathes life into the story of early Methodism so that it will breathe life into the church of the 21st century."

–Laceye C. Warner, Executive Vice-Dean of Duke Divinity School; author of *The Method of Our Mission* and *Grace to Lead* (with Kenneth L. Carder)

Revival

FAITH AS WESLEY LIVED IT

Revival

Faith as Wesley Lived It

Revival: Faith as Wesley Lived It
978-1-426-77884-1   *Also available as an eBook*

Revival: Faith as Wesley Lived It—Large Print Edition
978-1-630-88294-5

Revival: DVD
978-1-426-77682-3

Revival: Leader Guide
978-1-426-77883-4   *Also available as an eBook*

Revival: Youth Study Book
978-1-426-78868-0   *Also available as an eBook*

Revival: Children's Leader Guide
978-1-426-78871-0

For more information, visit www.AdamHamilton.org.

Also by Adam Hamilton

24 Hours That Changed the World

Christianity and World Religions

Christianity's Family Tree

Confronting the Controversies

Enough

Final Words from the Cross

Forgiveness

Leading Beyond the Walls

Love to Stay

Making Sense of the Bible

Not a Silent Night

Seeing Gray in a World of Black and White

Selling Swimsuits in the Arctic

The Journey

The Way

Unleashing the Word

When Christians Get It Wrong

Why?

ADAM HAMILTON

Revival

FAITH AS WESLEY LIVED IT

Abingdon Press / Nashville

REVIVAL: FAITH AS WESLEY LIVED IT

Copyright © 2014 Abingdon Press

All rights reserved.

This book is printed on acid-free, elemental chlorine-free paper.

ISBN 978-1-426-77884-1

All Scripture quotations, unless otherwise indicated, are taken from the New Revised Standard Version of the Bible, copyright 1989, Division of Christian Education of the National Council of the Churches of Christ in the United States of America. Used by permission. All rights reserved.

Scripture quotations marked (NIV) are taken from the Holy Bible, New International Version®, NIV®. Copyright © 1973, 1978, 1984, 2011 by Biblica, Inc.™ Used by permission of Zondervan. All rights reserved worldwide. www.zondervan.com. The "NIV" and "New International Version" are trademarks registered in the United States Patent and Trademark Office by Biblica, Inc.™

Hamilton, Adam, 1964-
  Revival : faith as Wesley lived it / Adam Hamilton.
    1 online resource.
  Includes bibliographical references.
  Description based on print version record and CIP data provided by publisher; resource not viewed.
  ISBN 978-1-4267-9387-5 (epub) -- ISBN 978-1-4267-7884-1 (pbk., adhesive-perfect binding : alk. paper) 1. Wesley, John, 1703-1791. 2. Christian life--Methodist authors. I. Title.
  BX8495.W5
  287.092--dc23

                    2014025519

15 16 17 18 19 20 21 22 23—10 9 8 7 6 5 4 3 2

MANUFACTURED IN THE UNITED STATES OF AMERICA

To Professor Richard Heitzenrater,
who instilled in me a love of
John Wesley and the early Methodists

Contents

Introduction

In every Christian's life, spiritual vitality or passion wanes over time. This is actually true in all aspects of our lives. In marriage, we slowly find that the fire diminishes if we're not intentional about revival in our love lives. This happens in friendships. It happens with our jobs—we call it burnout. In every part of our lives we need revival from time to time.

Recently I was given a beautiful flowering plant. When I remember to water it, the plant looks healthy and vibrant. But after a few days without water, it begins to wilt. Two weeks without water and its leaves become dry, brown, and brittle. In our spiritual lives we have seasons when we are blooming and bearing fruit, when our vitality is high. But when we neglect our spiritual lives, we begin to wilt. When we have prolonged periods of inattention to the spiritual life, our faith goes dormant. We may go through the motions of Christian life, but the vitality is gone.

We don't often use the word *revival* anymore. For many, the idea of revival is quaint at best; at worst, it calls up images of tent meetings where silver-tongued preachers take advantage of gullible believers. But the word, based on the Latin *re-vivere*, means to reinvigorate, to restore to life, to become strong and healthy after a period of decline, to renew or revitalize.

I know there are times when my faith has ebbed, times when I have become too busy to tend to my spiritual life. I think this is true for each of us. Perhaps this is one of those times for you. If your spiritual life were a flowering plant, is it currently blooming and fully alive, or is it wilting and perhaps even dying?

What is true for us as individuals is true of churches, denominations, and even revival movements within the Christian faith. These, too, eventually lose their spiritual vitality. Even in the New Testament period, the writer of the Book of Revelation noted that some of the churches in Asia had lost their "first love" and become "lukewarm." The same might be said of the denominational families that sprang out of the Wesleyan movement. I believe the seeds of our revival, and the revival of Christianity today, are to be found in the story of our beginning.

In preparing to write this book, I went to England to retrace the steps of John Wesley and the beginnings of Methodism. Methodism started as a revival of Christianity in Britain, but it also spread like wildfire across America. What, I wondered, are the things early Methodists did that might help twenty-first-century Christians rediscover a vital faith?

There have been many excellent books written about John Wesley and the eighteenth-century evangelical revival he led. Likewise there have been several fine books on the beliefs and practices of United Methodists. What I'm hoping to do in this book is a bit different. I will describe key events from the life of John Wesley, then seek to show how, in those events, we find lessons for our own spiritual journey. I hope to capture some of the most important convictions, qualities, and essential practices of Wesley and the early Methodists. Ultimately my goal is not simply to teach history but to help us find revival in our own hearts and lives.

It should also be said here that the eighteenth-century evangelical revival Wesley launched was not only the result of God's work through John Wesley, but God's work through so many others, chief among whom was John's younger brother Charles. I had intended to prepare an entire chapter on Charles Wesley and his contribution to the revival, but ultimately I chose to focus solely on John's life and faith, with only a nod here or there to Charles. This choice was necessitated in part by the length and kind of book I sought to write. I encourage the reader to take the time to explore Charles Wesley's life, faith, ministry, and hymn writing. His contribution to the Wesleyan revival was incalculable, even though our attention is typically focused on his brother, as it will be in this volume.

In my research for this book, I reread many of Wesley's sermons as well as a number of outstanding books on Wesley and eighteenth-century Methodism. I was grateful for the opportunity to spend time with Duke professor Dr. Richard Heitzenrater, one of the preeminent living Wesley scholars. My own congregation allowed me a sabbatical leave to study Wesley's life. In the summer of 2013, with the help of a Lilly Endowment Clergy Renewal Grant and the assistance of Educational Opportunities Tours, I traveled to England with a film crew to retrace Wesley's life and the emergence of Methodism. Bishop Scott Jones, himself a Wesley scholar, accompanied me and served as my guide. Our spouses, LaVon and Mary Lou, joined us along with videographers Lee Rudeen and Natalie Cleveland.

After writing the first draft of this book I asked a number of leading Wesley scholars to read it to see if I had accurately captured the facts of Wesley's life and the development of the Methodist revival. Among the scholars were Professors Richard Heitzenrater, Randy Maddox, and Hal Knight, as well as Bishop Scott Jones and Dr. Geordan Hammond of the Manchester Wesley Research Centre in England. I'm grateful to them. They identified errors I had incorporated from other sources and conclusions that are no longer held by most Wesley scholars. Where errors remain, they are my own.

I've written a section at the end of each chapter designed to take you to a key location in Wesley's life, and I'm including photos I took so you can make the trip vicariously with me.

In addition to writing this book, we've prepared a series of videos that you may want to use as part of a group or personal study. For each chapter, a ten- to fifteen-minute video takes you as viewers to the places described, starting with Wesley's childhood home at Epworth and ending in the room where Wesley died at his home next to City Road Chapel.

Ultimately I wrote this book because I believe that by reclaiming the faith, heart, and practices of John Wesley and the early Methodists, we can rediscover the best parts of our own hearts and churches, and in so doing we might help spark a revival of Christianity in our time.

1.

Precursors to Revival

Epworth

To the angel of the church in Ephesus write: . . . "I know your works, your toil and your patient endurance. . . . But I have this against you, that you have abandoned the love you had at first. Remember then from what you have fallen; repent, and do the works you did at first."

(Revelation 2:1a, 2a, 4-5a)

1.

Precursors to Revival

Epworth

We often look at the Book of Revelation as a guide to the end times, but that's not really how or why it was written. Revelation was written near the end of the first century to seven churches in Asia Minor, which comprises much of modern-day Turkey. These churches had once been dynamic centers of Christianity. Among them was the church at Ephesus on the coast of the Aegean Sea. Paul lived in Ephesus for more than two years. John the disciple lived out his days in the vicinity of Ephesus. At least one early church tradition suggests that Mary the mother of Jesus spent her final years there as well. It was once a lively, passionate church.

By the time Revelation was written, Ephesus, along with some of the other churches of Revelation, had lost its vitality. Christ, speaking to the author of Revelation, noted that the believers in Laodicea had become "lukewarm" (Revelation 3:16) and the Christians at Ephesus had lost their first love (2:4). These Christians were busy, but their activities had not produced spiritual vitality. In Revelation, the Lord told them the key to their spiritual revival was to "do the works you did at first" (2:5).

This pattern of declining spiritual vitality was not unique to the churches of Revelation. We can see it throughout the Old Testament, as the Israelites pledged their devotion and allegiance to God, then gradually fell away. Crisis came, and they cried out for help. God delivered them, and once more they pledged their allegiance to God. But within a generation they fell away once more. The history of Christianity is much the same. Pastor Robert Robinson rightly captured this in his 1758 hymn "Come, Thou Fount of Every Blessing" when he wrote, "Prone to wander, Lord, I feel it, prone to leave the God I love. . . ."[1]

In my own life, even as a pastor, I've had seasons when I experienced spiritual burnout. In my flurry of activity I had stopped or greatly reduced the spiritual practices that can open our hearts to God's Spirit. I had the outward appearance of spiritual vitality, but inwardly I felt empty. Sometimes I was so busy doing things pastors must do that I was not aware my spiritual vitality was waning. Yet often in those times I, or those closest to me, could sense a diminution of the fruit of the Spirit in my life. There was a reduction of "love, joy, peace, patience, kindness, generosity, faithfulness, gentleness, and self-control" (Galatians 5:22-23) in my heart, words, and actions.

I've visited many churches where the people seem to be going through the motions of Christianity but lack the fruit of the Spirit. To them I believe the Lord would say, "I know your works, your toil and your patient endurance. . . . But I have this against you, that you have abandoned the love you had at first."

The early eighteenth century was a time when spiritual vitality was ebbing in many parts of the Church of England. As a young man at Oxford, John Wesley could feel it, not only in the church and university but in his own soul. He felt there must be more to the Christian life than what he knew. Wesley longed for something more. It was in his longing that the seeds of the Methodist revival were sown.

Responding to the Times

To understand John Wesley's thoughts and beliefs, we need to know something of the world into which he was born, for it was that world that shaped the Methodist movement.

For two hundred years leading up to Wesley's birth, Europe had been in the throes of religious conflict. In 1517, Martin Luther nailed his Ninety-Five Theses to the doors of the Castle Church in Wittenberg, Germany. His protest against the practice of selling indulgences in the Catholic Church, and against a host of other common practices of the church at that time, set off a revolution. Lines were drawn between those who were loyal to the Pope and remained Roman Catholic, and those who joined Luther's protest and became Protestants.

In England, the more immediate source of conflict was the desire by King Henry VIII to produce a male heir. He sought to have his marriage annulled so that he could marry again, and when that effort failed he severed ties between the English church and Rome. By 1534, Henry had himself declared the Supreme Head of the Church of England, and by 1536 an act was passed to disband most of the monasteries and convents.

Though Henry's Church of England was no longer tied to the Roman Catholic Church, its theology and practice remained far more Catholic than those of the other Protestant countries at the time. But after Henry's death, his son Edward VI and Edward's advisors led the church toward a closer alignment with what was becoming mainstream Protestantism. This represented a significant shift in Christian practice in England. Edward died before his sixteenth birthday, and after some palace intrigue his half-sister Mary I came to the throne.

Mary I, a staunch Roman Catholic, restored the Church of England to Catholic doctrine and practice and to the Pope's authority. She ordered that prominent Anglican bishops and Protestant leaders in the church be put to death, mostly burned at the stake, for which she is forever remembered as "Bloody Mary." You can imagine the religious upheaval that this caused. Mary was succeeded by Elizabeth I, who ruled for nearly forty-five years. Elizabeth returned England to a firmly Protestant path. Her reign, as regards religion, is remembered for seeking compromise between various Protestant factions as well as an occasional nod to Catholic sensibilities.

Elizabeth died in 1603 and was followed by James VI, the king of Scotland, who also became James I, the king of England and Ireland. Like Elizabeth, James sought a balance between Catholicism and Protestantism. He supported a new translation of the Bible into English, which was formally known as the Authorized Version of the Bible but came to be known as the King James Version.

By that time, a movement had arisen among the more ardent Protestants, who came to be known as Puritans. Puritans opposed the vestiges of Catholicism in the church and believed the reformation of the English church had never gone far enough. James's successor, Charles I, supported "high church" forms of Anglicanism, married a Roman Catholic, and in a host of other ways alienated Puritans and many others. During his reign the English Civil War broke out. In 1649, King Charles was executed, and England became a Commonwealth.

More religious upheaval followed, as the Puritans and their leader Oliver Cromwell enforced their strong aversion to anything Catholic. With Cromwell's death in 1658, England had had enough of radical Puritanism, and Charles II, son of Charles I, was welcomed back as King of England in what became known as the Restoration. By 1662 the Church of England was restored, with its Book of Common Prayer, Articles of Religion, bishops, and other practices.

As part of the Restoration, pastors were required to submit to an Act of Uniformity. Over two thousand pastors refused to comply. They were forced out of their churches, forbidden from traveling within five miles of their former churches, and prevented from teaching in schools. Even after the Restoration, conflict between the Church of England and its dissenters—the Puritans and later the Calvinists—continued, lasting into the eighteenth century.

Because of this two hundred–year period of religious upheaval, many among the English people had grown weary of religion. The Enlightenment, a movement in which reason and scientific rationalism raised questions of religious traditions and beliefs, was further eroding religious fervor, particularly in the universities. The waning of religious sentiment and the rise of Enlightenment philosophies provided a perfect seedbed for the eighteenth-century revival in which Wesley would play so prominent a part.

The Power of a Praying Mother

John Wesley was born in Epworth, England, on June 17, 1703, to Samuel and Susanna Wesley.[2] Epworth is a small town about 150 miles north of London and 130 miles south of the Scottish border. Downtown Epworth today looks very much like it did when Wesley was there. The Red Lion Inn, where Wesley stayed when he visited town after his father's death, is still open. The "market cross," upon whose steps John frequently preached, still stands. (Market crosses were erected in the center of most towns across England, in part as a visible reminder that Christ watched over the townspeople as they conducted their business.) The home where John Wesley grew up and the church where he was baptized remain as Epworth's primary tourist attractions.

John's father, Samuel, devoted nearly forty years to serving that church, St. Andrew's Church in Epworth. Portions of the building, which recently has been remodeled, are said to date back to the 1100s. Samuel baptized John and his siblings at the font in this church. You can still see the chalice from which Samuel offered eight-year-old John his first Eucharist. After John's ordination, he served this same church as curate (essentially an associate) under his father. Samuel, after his death, was buried in the graveyard next to the church. Wesley famously preached from atop his father's grave when the new priest at St. Andrew's would not allow him to preach inside the church.

Though Samuel's preaching shaped his children, clearly it was John's mother, Susanna, who had the greatest impact on their faith. She is often referred to as the "mother of Methodism."

Susanna was the beautiful, intelligent daughter of a popular Puritan minister in London. He insisted that his daughter receive a classical education, something most unusual at the time. She was a brilliant woman who later insisted that her own daughters learn to read, write, and pursue their education.

Samuel and Susanna married November 11, 1688. When Samuel became rector (priest in charge) of St. Andrew's Church sometime around 1695, the couple moved to the rectory (parsonage). The original rectory was destroyed by fire in 1709 when John was just five years old, a story we'll consider in more detail shortly. The house that currently stands, built when John was six years old, was the Wesley family home until Samuel died in 1735 and the home was given to the new rector, at which time Susanna went to live with her children.

It was in the kitchen of this "new" rectory that Susanna educated her children for six hours a day. It was where she held family devotions early on Sunday evenings. One time when Samuel was in London and the associate rector replacing him was a rather dull preacher, some of the townsfolk asked if they could join Susanna's Sunday devotions. As a result, more people began coming to her lessons than were attending church at St. Andrew's to hear the associate rector preach.

The associate, a Mr. Inman, complained to Samuel about the services Susanna was holding in their home. Samuel wrote asking her to stop, since it was considered scandalous that a woman would be, in essence, preaching to the congregation. Susanna's response to her husband made the case for why the meetings were appropriate, then ended with these words:

> If you do, after all, think fit to dissolve this assembly, do not tell me that you desire me to do it, for that will not satisfy my conscience; but send me your positive command, in such full and express terms as may absolve me from all guilt and punishment, for neglecting this opportunity of doing good, when you and I shall appear before the great and awful tribunal of our LORD JESUS CHRIST.[3]

After that, Samuel didn't say another word about the services!

Susanna had a profound continuing influence on the faith of her children. Her writings included an extended catechism, prepared for her children. What's remarkable is how intentional she was about forming the faith of her children and continuing to invest in their faith when they became adults.

John's mother was a commanding presence in his life. He sought her wisdom. He valued her insights. There were many occasions when he changed his mind about some matter of leadership owing to her intervention. In one case, a layman had begun preaching, and John was against having any but ordained clergy preach. Susanna challenged her son to listen to the man preach and to see that God was working through him. Wesley did as Susanna suggested, and from that time on, lay preachers became an important feature of Methodism.

Among the beautiful things Susanna Wesley did with her children was to spend one hour a week with each child, asking about their faith, their fears, their hopes and dreams, the state of their souls. This loving activity was to shape Wesley's later practice of asking Methodists to meet together weekly in small groups to enquire about one another's progress in the faith.

Susanna was not what today we would consider to be the perfect mother. For example, she believed in the importance of breaking a child's spirit and in children not being allowed to cry. Today these practices would be considered harsh, though in her own time they were considered good parenting principles.

What strikes me in reading Susanna's words, and the words of her children about her, was how important her faith, life, and prayers were for the Methodist revival that two of her sons would lead. When Charles Wesley, John's hymn-writing brother, was asked to what he attributed his conversion in college and his newfound spiritual vitality, he did not hesitate; he believed it was because of his mother's prayers. Think of 2 Timothy 1:5, in which Paul writes to Timothy, "I am reminded of your sincere faith, a faith that lived first in your grandmother Lois and your mother Eunice and now, I am sure, lives in you." For John and Charles, as for Timothy, their sincere faith lived first in their father and mother. Both parents had a profound impact upon the faith of their children, but Susanna's influence arguably was greater.

At the age of seventy-three, Susanna Wesley lay in bed approaching death. John noted in his journal of July 30, 1742, "I found my mother on the borders of eternity. But she had no doubt or fear nor any desire but (as soon as God should call) 'to depart and be with Christ.'" Her last request of her children was, "Children, as soon as I am released, sing a psalm of praise to God."[4] She died later that day, and on Sunday John preached at her funeral, where a tremendous crowd had gathered to celebrate her life. Susanna Wesley changed the world by shaping the heart and faith of her children and by her wise counsel and persistent prayers and encouragement. It is not an exaggeration to say that there would have been no Methodist movement had it not been for the faith and prayers of Susanna Wesley. Susanna was buried at the Bunhill Fields cemetery in London. Years later, right across the street, John Wesley would build his home and City Road Chapel, which became Methodism's mother church. From his study Wesley could look out and see his mother's grave. She continued to inspire him years after she had died.

A Humble, Listening, Catholic Spirit

If John Wesley learned about faith from his mother, he learned how to deal with disagreements from his father and grandfathers.

In many ways those two generations of Wesley's family reflected the religious conflicts of the time. John's grandfathers on both his mother's and his father's sides were dissenters from the established Anglican Church and had been strongly influenced by the Puritans; his parents were committed Anglicans deeply devoted to the established church with its high-church liturgy. John's grandparents refused to embrace the Book of Common Prayer and had been cast out of their churches as a result of the Act of Uniformity; his parents embraced the Book of Common Prayer and sought to ensure its use in the churches they served.

How did these family conflicts affect John Wesley? Wesley adopted a posture that is often called the *via media*—a middle way—that found truth on both sides of the theological divide. He was a cleric of the Church of England, yet he embraced many Puritan expressions of faith. He worshiped in the high-church tradition, yet he opened preaching houses that were filled with rousing hymn singing and little liturgy. Wesley had the ability to value and listen to people on opposite sides of the theological divide, to find the truth each possessed, and to chart a middle way, embracing the best of both sides.

Spiritual Mentors

A precursor to our own revival is often the prayers of our parents or grandparents. I remember that years ago, one of the founding members of The United Methodist Church of the Resurrection, the church where I serve, told me how she came to faith. She had been away from the church for more than thirty years, but her mother kept sending letters and telling her she needed God and needed the church. She told me, "I was so irritated that my mother was still trying to tell me how to live my life. Here I was, a grandmother, and she still was telling me what to do!" But as her mother became ill and later died, my friend could not stop thinking about those letters and the words of her mother. It was her mother's witness that led her back to church, where she experienced her own revival of faith.

For those of us who are parents, or aunts or uncles, we have a major role to play in the faith of our children and grandchildren, nieces and nephews. As my own children were growing up, I would pray at their bedside on my knees every night. I knew it was likely that one day they would turn away from their faith as they tried to discover who they were apart from being the preacher's daughters. But I hoped they would never forget their father praying next to their bedside at night, or their mother reading Scripture to them and telling them about her faith. Do you pray with your children and grandchildren, nieces and nephews? Do you take time to talk with them about faith? Do you write them notes about your faith? Are you spiritually mentoring these children? That's what Susanna did with her children, and the Methodist revival and all who trace their lineage through it are the fruit of her witness.

Not long ago I went to visit Marilyn, the mother of a longtime friend. She was in a hospice approaching death. I'd known her since I was fourteen. We had a wonderful visit as both of her sons looked on. Her youngest son, my friend, is a member of my congregation. Before I left she said, "I want to thank you for something." I asked, "What's that, Marilyn?" She said, "Thank you for bringing my son back to church. He wasn't going until he reconnected with you and began attending again. That means so very much to me." As my friend and I walked to the car I told him, "You know, I think your mom said that for your benefit. She wanted you to know how much it means to her that you are a follower of Christ, and she doesn't want you to fall away after she's gone." I'm guessing many of you had mothers or fathers, grandmothers or grandfathers, aunts or uncles who prayed you back to church, and you didn't even know it.

In his introduction to *Explanatory Notes upon the New Testament*, Wesley wrote these words that capture his spirit so well:

> Would to God that all the party names and unscriptural phrases and forms which have divided the Christian world were forgot; and that we might all agree to sit down together as humble, loving disciples, at the feet of our common Master, to hear his word, to imbibe his Spirit, and to transcribe his life in our own![5]

In one of his most famous sermons, "Catholic Spirit," Wesley wrote, "Though we can't think alike, may we not love alike? May we not be of one heart, though we are not of one opinion? Without all doubt, we may."[6] Wesley was calling his hearers to listen to those with whom they disagreed and to focus on what they shared in common. He was teaching them (and us!) to build bridges rather than walls. The word *catholic* is a bit confusing to some, but in this context it simply means "universal." It conveys the sense that the church, the body of Christ, is made up not only of people who are in my denomination or tribe but of all who call upon the name of Christ, even if they disagree on this or that point of doctrine.

The twenty-first century is as polarized as eighteenth-century England. We're not Tories and Whigs, conformists and dissenters, Anglicans and Puritans; we're Republicans and Democrats, fundamentalists and progressives, liberals and conservatives. Yet divisiveness and conflict drain us of our spiritual vitality and leave many today longing for a different approach, an approach like Wesley's catholic spirit.

How do we do embrace such an approach today? Paul described it when he admonished the believers in Philippi, who themselves were divided, "Do nothing from selfish ambition or conceit, but in humility regard others as better than yourselves. Let each of you look not to your own interests, but to the interests of others. Let the same mind be in you that was in Christ Jesus" (Philippians 2:3-5). To the Christians at Corinth, who also were deeply divided, Paul noted that love was the defining characteristic of Christian life, and then he went on to describe the character of Christian love: "Love is patient; love is kind; love is not envious or boastful or arrogant or rude. It does not insist on its own way; it is not irritable or resentful; it does not rejoice in wrongdoing, but rejoices in the truth. It bears all things, believes all things, hopes all things, endures all things" (1 Corinthians 13:4-7).

Having a spirit like Wesley's today means that we assume the best of others, not the worst. We give them the benefit of the doubt. We speak well of others, not poorly. We treat them as we hope to be treated. We listen more and talk less. We walk in other people's shoes and try to understand what they believe and why. This does not mean we give up our convictions, but it does mean we test them. I've found that, after listening to another person's point of view, some ideas I was sure of were not nearly so convincing. I've found that, on more than one occasion, views that seemed utterly indefensible actually were quite convincing when I moved beyond my assumptions and took the time to listen.

I've also learned that it's easy to be adamantly opposed to a viewpoint or position—be it theological, ethical, or political—when no one I deeply care about holds such views. But as I get to know those with views different from my own and come to care about them and consider them my friends, it is hard to be adamantly opposed to their views.

Among the defining characteristics of the Christian life are humility, grace, and love. The test of our faith comes in how we respond to others and how willing we are to listen to, learn from, and love them.

On a recent Sunday when I was on vacation, a neighbor invited me to worship at his Pentecostal church. I think there were sixteen of us in worship that day, including the preacher's family. The preacher spoke without notes, in what seemed to be an almost completely extemporaneous message. I could not discern an outline or order to the sermon. It was passionate, nonlinear, and all over the map. I tried taking notes, but I could not follow the logical progression. As he preached, however, there came a point when I felt God's nudge. When the preacher got to the end he said, "Well, somewhere in all that, something should have spoken to you!" And he was right. Had I gone to the service with a critical spirit, a smug heart, or a feeling of superiority, I would have received nothing that day. Instead I left having felt that God had spoken to me.

We have forgotten how to listen, as individuals, as churches, and as a nation. Liberals and conservatives, Republicans and Democrats, progressives and fundamentalists find it easy to demonize others. The mark of those early Methodists, and a key element of personal and corporate revival in the twenty-first century, is a willingness to see the good in others, hold our positions with humility, and treat others with respect. It is a willingness to make our hearts pliable in God's hands. It is a willingness to follow the highest calling of Christians, which is both the prerequisite and the goal of revival: love.

The Importance of Perseverance

This leads me to one final lesson John Wesley learned from his family, and largely from his father. It was a lesson that would be essential in the revival he would lead: When suffering, tragedy, and opposition come, don't turn away; turn to God. And don't give up.

Samuel and Susanna knew sorrow, adversity, and pain. They lost nine of their children at childbirth or in early childhood. How many couples would have turned away from God under these circumstances? Instead, they found hope and strength. They didn't blame God. They trusted that God was holding their children and wouldn't let go.

Samuel was often in debt. He had a wife and children to care for on a rector's salary. If you read Susanna Wesley's letters, you'll find that many of them deal with the lack of money and the financial stress in the Wesley home.[7]

In addition, Samuel had a knack for upsetting some of his parishioners. He lived in a region where people resented the king, yet Samuel supported the king. Epworth was a rural area, yet Samuel and Susanna, both with fine educations, felt more at home in the city. At times, Samuel seemed to lack tact in his approach with the congregation. For these and other reasons, some of his parishioners simply didn't like him. (Any pastor reading this can relate to Samuel!)

One time, for example, Samuel had upset one of his parishioners to whom he owed money. The man demanded immediate repayment, knowing Wesley couldn't pay, and Samuel was thrown into debtors' prison. The congregation likely could have found a way to pay their preacher's debt, but it was three months before the bishop bailed him out! While Samuel was in debtor's prison, he wrote to his children in good humor, telling them his imprisonment was an opportunity to minister to his fellow "jailbirds." Clearly, we can see a quality in Samuel that his son John later displayed: He didn't give up in the face of opposition or adversity.

In 1709, when John was five years old, someone set fire to the thatched roof of their house while the family slept. (Samuel was convinced it was someone in the congregation.) The house burned so quickly that the Wesleys barely escaped with their lives. When they got out, they took a count and found that one child was missing. It was John. Samuel tried to rush back in and get him, but the house was engulfed in flames. He knelt in prayer with his children, commending little John to God's care. At that moment one of the townsfolk noticed John standing just inside a window. A man climbed onto someone's shoulders, and they pulled John to safety just as the roof collapsed.

Susanna and later John came to believe that God had saved him for some special purpose. Quoting Zechariah 3:2, Susanna called John a "brand plucked from the fire." John understood his life to have been spared by God for some great purpose, and this sense of destiny was what he believed he had found in leading the people called Methodists.

Every pastor receives an occasional unkind letter or e-mail from a parishioner. But Samuel and Susanna Wesley had lost children at birth, Samuel had been thrown in jail, and later he had watched his house burn down, all the while facing opposition from parishioners. If it were me, I think I might have called it quits. Yet after each of these incidents Samuel returned to the pulpit of St. Andrew's, and he continued preaching there until his death in 1735. He did not give up in the face of opposition.

John's unwillingness to quit in the face of hardship, learned by watching his father, would be an important part of the Methodist revival. It is the key to any great work. Winston Churchill said the same thing in his famous speech at the Harrow School in October 1941. At the time the Nazis appeared invincible, but Churchill declared, "Never give in, never give in, never, never, never—in nothing, great or small, large or petty—never give in!"[8]

Consider St. Paul, who was imprisoned many times, beaten with rods, shipwrecked, and left for dead, yet he refused to give up. I love the way he viewed adversity and suffering: "We also boast in our sufferings, knowing that suffering produces endurance, and endurance produces character, and character produces hope, and hope does not disappoint us, because God's love has been poured into our hearts through the Holy Spirit that has been given to us" (Romans 5:3-5).

Life is hard. We will face opposition. There will come trouble and suffering. Some will give in. Some will turn away from God. Some will throw in the towel. But John Wesley learned from his father that you don't run, you don't turn from your faith, and you don't give up.

There were three precursors to revival that we've noted in this chapter: Wesley had parents who prayed for and spiritually mentored him; he had a teachable spirit—a "catholic spirit"—that was humble and willing to see the important truths on both sides of the theological divide; and he learned perseverance in the face of opposition. These features of Wesley's early life were important precursors to the eighteenth-century Methodist revival.

What to See in Epworth

Photos by Adam Hamilton unless otherwise noted

Epworth is in Lincolnshire, a little over three hours' drive from London. A small town of less than four thousand residents, Epworth is sometimes skipped on tours of Wesley's England because it is out of the way. But a visit there is a must, in my opinion, if you are retracing Wesley's life and the birth of Methodism. If you are in a small group, consider staying at the Red Lion Inn, where there are thirteen rooms and a great pub with good food. Wesley himself would stay at the Red Lion when he returned to Epworth in the years following his father's death. (www.redlionepworth.co.uk). Just across the street from the Red Lion Inn is the market cross where Wesley stood and preached on visits to the town. A plaque commemorates his preaching there.

The Red Lion Inn and market cross at Epworth

Just off the square, a short walk from the Red Lion Inn, is St. Andrew's Church, the Anglican church where Samuel Wesley, John's father, served as rector from around 1695 to his death in 1735 (www.standrewsepworth.co.uk). Parts of the church building may date back to the 1100s.

St. Andrew's Church

The building has recently been renovated, but inside you can still see the baptismal font where both John and Charles were baptized. John served as curate (essentially an associate to his father) for a short while after his ordination. Spend time at St. Andrew's praying and reflecting upon how your own faith has been shaped by the Wesley boys who grew up in this church.

Baptismal font

Step outside the church, and nearby you'll find the grave of Samuel Wesley. Samuel's grave was the site of a famous incident, when John visited Epworth and the new and somewhat insecure rector did not allow him to preach in St. Andrew's. Later that day, John stood on his father's grave and preached to a crowd significantly larger than had attended St. Andrew's in the morning.

Samuel Wesley's grave

You will want to visit the Epworth Old Rectory (the parsonage). This home was built in 1709 after the first rectory burned down, the incident that nearly cost John his life. This "new" old rectory is now owned by the World Methodist Council and is being restored. A guide will tell you all about the place. If you can spare a donation the council will be grateful, as they are doing important work on a minimal budget (www.epwortholdrectory.org.uk).

Epworth Old Rectory

2.
A Longing for Holiness
Oxford

Therefore prepare your minds for action; discipline yourselves; set all your hope on the grace that Jesus Christ will bring you when he is revealed. Like obedient children, do not be conformed to the desires that you formerly had in ignorance. Instead, as he who called you is holy, be holy yourselves in all your conduct; for it is written, "You shall be holy, for I am holy."

(1 Peter 1:13-16)

2.
A Longing for Holiness
Oxford

At the age of ten, John Wesley began his formal education at Charterhouse School in London, a school whose excellence pleased his father. John attended on scholarship; his family could not otherwise afford the tuition. Two decades after matriculating, Wesley would write of his spiritual life during this period at Charterhouse:

> The next six or seven years were spent at school; where, outward restraints being removed, I was much more negligent than before even of outward duties, and almost continually guilty of outward sins, which I knew to be such, though they were not scandalous in the eye of the world. However, I still read the Scriptures, and said my prayers, morning and evening. And what I now hoped to be saved by, was, (1) *Not being so bad as other people*; (2) *having still a kindness for religion*; and (3) *reading the Bible, going to church, and saying my prayers.*[1]

Upon finishing his studies at Charterhouse, Wesley was ready to enter the university. In 1720, at the age of seventeen, he began his studies at Christ Church, one of the largest and most prestigious colleges that make up Oxford University.

For most of his undergraduate studies, Wesley was like many college students. Biographer Kenneth Collins notes that Wesley "frequented the coffee house, rowed on the river, and played backgammon, billiards, chess, cards, and tennis."[2] Samuel Badcock, an eighteenth-century minister and writer who knew the Wesley family, described Wesley during his college years as "the very sensible collegian, baffling every man by the subtleties of logic . . . a young fellow of the finest classical taste . . . with a turn for wit and humor."[3] In other words, Wesley was a normal college student!

Though his father was an Anglican priest, it was likely his mother who played a larger role in Wesley's decision to be ordained. John himself was feeling called to academia, but at Oxford most of the fellows were ordained priests, so being ordained would serve him well whether he would serve the church directly in a parish or indirectly through the university.

Half a Christian?

Shortly after completing his bachelor's degree in 1724, Wesley began work on both his master's degree and his ordination. As he prepared for ordination, John became more serious about his faith. Wesley noted that in 1725 he was "exceedingly affected" by reading Jeremy Taylor's *The Rule and Exercises of Holy Living*, a book first published in 1650.[4]

One theme of Taylor's work that seized Wesley's heart came from Paul's words in 1 Corinthians 10:31: "So, whether you eat or drink, or whatever you do, do everything for the glory of God." Taylor taught that "every action of nature becomes religious, and every meal is an act of worship . . . as well as an act of prayer."[5] Taylor's words challenged Wesley to see everything he did as being for the glory of God.

Another passage that challenged Wesley was one he had prayed thousands of times throughout his life. It was the doxology at the end of the Lord's Prayer: "For thine is the kingdom and the power and the glory." It struck Wesley that sin can lead us subconsciously to live a different prayer: "Mine is the kingdom and the power and the glory."[6]

Each of us knows the inner drive for affirmation, praise, recognition, and glory. I suspect this drive was intended by God to help us do things that are good and praiseworthy and try our hardest and to do our best. We feel a certain pride in a job well done. We feel good when someone notices what we've accomplished. Awards, honors, even thank-you notes are positive affirmations. But when recognition or glory becomes our primary motivation, we've strayed from God's path and stepped onto the path of narcissism and pride.

To counteract this tendency, Jeremy Taylor suggested that Christians start each day, and begin each action, with prayer. You may be familiar with a form of prayer sometimes called "breath prayers." These are short prayers, often taken directly from Scripture, that can be prayed in one breath and repeated throughout the day. Psalm 115:1 is an excellent example: "Not to us, O LORD, not to us, but to your name give glory." Praying these words in the morning when you wake up and throughout the day will begin to form and shape your heart and your intention.

Wesley noted, after reading Taylor's work, "Instantly I resolved to dedicate all my life to God, all my thoughts, and words, and actions."[7] He was twenty-three years old, and his decision would be pivotal to the Wesleyan revival. The idea of doing everything for the glory of God would become a mark of a Methodist, as it should be of any Christian.

In 1726, Wesley began reading the devotional classic *The Imitation of Christ*, written by the fourteenth-century monk Thomas à Kempis. Today, nearly seven hundred years after it was written, the book still sells thousands of copies every year. Wesley read it devotionally again and again. This is what he said the book taught him: "I saw that giving even all my life to God . . . would profit me nothing, unless I gave my heart, yea, all my heart to him."[8] This reinforced Wesley's primary goal in life: To do everything for the glory of God and to love God with all that was within him.

In 1730, at age twenty-seven, Wesley read William Law's recently published book A *Serious Call to a Devout and Holy Life*. It convinced Wesley "of the absolute impossibility of being half a Christian."[9] He was determined to be "all-devoted to God," what he called an "altogether Christian."

Wesley's concern not to be "half a Christian" would continue to plague him and would shape his ministry and preaching. Eleven years later, at age thirty-eight, Wesley would preach one of his most famous sermons before a gathering of professors and students at St. Mary's Church in Oxford. With evangelical fervor he implored his listeners not to be satisfied with being an "almost Christian" but to become an "altogether Christian." Through a series of questions he laid out what it means to be an altogether Christian:

> Is the love of God shed abroad in your heart? Can you cry out, "My God, and my all"? Do you desire nothing but him? Are you happy in God? Is he your glory, your delight, your crown of rejoicing? And is this commandment written in your heart, "that he who loveth God love his brother also"? Do you then love your neighbour as yourself? Do you love every man, even your enemies, even the enemies of God, as your own soul? As Christ loved you? Yea, dost thou believe that Christ loved thee, and gave himself for thee? Hast thou faith in his blood? Believest thou the Lamb of God hath taken away *thy* sins, and cast them as a stone into the depth of

the sea? That he hath blotted out the handwriting that was against *thee*, taking it out of the way, nailing it to his cross? Hast *thou* indeed redemption through his blood, even the remission of *thy* sins? And doth his Spirit bear witness with *thy* spirit, that thou art a child of God?[10]

The rhetorical questions, asked rapid-fire and with passion, remind me of preaching in the African American tradition. There's no time to respond to the individual question before the next is asked, but the weight of all the questions is meant to elicit a resounding "Yes!" At core, altogether Christians seek to love God and neighbor (the two great commandments that Jesus said summarize the Law and the Prophets); to trust in the forgiveness and grace made available through Christ to all who believe; and to welcome and experience the confirming witness of the Holy Spirit.

As Wesley read Jeremy Taylor, Thomas à Kempis, William Law, and others, he sensed that there was more to faith and holiness than he had known before. He found an increasing desire kindled in his heart for that something more. He longed to be an altogether Christian.

That's also how it works in our lives. We become aware that there is something more, perhaps by worshiping, reading books, studying Scripture, or being in small groups with other Christians. Based on these experiences, we find ourselves dissatisfied with our spiritual lives and longing to wade into the deeper waters of Christian faith. This, too, is a precursor to revival.

Pursuing the Christian Life

In 1726, while working toward his master's degree and ordination, Wesley was elected a fellow of Lincoln College, Oxford. To be a fellow of an Oxford college meant to be a faculty member with teaching responsibilities. Other responsibilities included research, writing, mentoring students, preaching in chapel, moderating debates, and serving as part of the governing board. Fellows were given lodging and meal privileges, and there was a certain prestige that came with the position. Though Wesley was no longer a fellow after he married in 1751 (fellows were, at the time, required to be single), to his death he referred to himself as a "sometime fellow of Lincoln College."

In February 1727, John Wesley received his master's degree, and in August he left Oxford for a period of time to serve as curate for his father in Epworth. In 1728, he was ordained a priest (having previously been ordained a deacon in 1725). For nearly fifteen months after his ordination, with brief intermissions, he served with his father at St. Andrew's Church in Epworth and at nearby Wroot, a parish that was yoked with Epworth. During this period, John's younger brother Charles wrote to him from Christ Church in Oxford, where Charles was studying. In his letters, Charles decried spiritual life on campus, saying that if students were serious about pursuing the Christian faith at Oxford they would receive no small amount of ribbing.

Charles had invited a friend, William Morgan, to seek to grow in faith with him. In 1729, John returned to Oxford for the summer, and Charles asked his older brother to serve as a spiritual mentor. That summer, John, Charles, and William Morgan met together from time to time for prayer and conversations about faith.

The following November, Wesley returned to Oxford to resume teaching responsibilities at Lincoln College, lecturing in Greek, logic, and philosophy. It was sometime that winter that John, Charles, William Morgan, and a fourth student, Bob Kirkham, began meeting multiple times each week, studying the classics on weekdays and the spiritual life on Sundays. They also attended chapel services and weekly Eucharist. It was these regular gatherings of Professor Wesley with three college students, seeking to become altogether

Christians under John's tutelage, that Wesley would later call the "first rise of Methodism."[11]

It's worth noting that Methodism started on a college campus in what today we would call campus ministry. Wesley's ministry at Oxford never had large numbers of students involved, but the small numbers who were involved birthed a movement that changed the world.

At the church I serve, we look for ways to encourage our college students when they go off to school. We send care packages around the time of finals with notes of encouragement and treats. We plan activities when they come back from school for summer break. And we hire some of them as interns during the summer to be mentored and serve in our ministry, recognizing that passionate and dedicated college students have amazing potential to change the world, as Wesley did.

It was at Oxford, as John met with these college students, that the small group element of Methodism had its beginnings as well. Of course, the practice of meeting regularly to grow in grace and encourage each other was not new, but was deeply rooted in the experience of the earliest church. In Acts 2:42 we read, "They devoted themselves to the apostles' teaching and fellowship, to the breaking of bread and the prayers," and in Acts 2:46 we learn that those meetings took place in the temple and in homes. In Chapter 4, we'll read more about the importance of small groups in the Methodist revival.

Some of the most powerful spiritual experiences of my life have come in small groups. In my current small group, I'm a participant, not a leader. We meet for two hours each week, eating, then praying, then holding a study of some kind, usually based either on a book about Christian life and faith or a book of the Bible. The people in my small group are an important part of my life. They encourage me, hold me accountable, challenge me, and teach me.

All of us need friends. At Church of the Resurrection we call them "stretcher bearers," harkening back to the people who brought their paralyzed friend to Jesus on a stretcher, as recounted in Mark 2:1-5. Jesus was teaching in a house at the time, and when the crowd prevented them from getting close, they hoisted their friend to the rooftop, tore the roof off the house, and lowered him before Jesus to be healed. Oh, to have friends who would go to such lengths for us!

For Wesley and his friends, being in a small group meant more than fellowship and study. In the summer of 1730, William Morgan suggested they begin visiting prisoners in Oxford to fulfill Christ's call in the Parable of the Sheep and the Goats (Matthew 25:31-46). Within a year the group was calling on the elderly, caring for the poor, and working with low-income children, going so far as to hire a teacher to help with the education of the children. These initiatives were the beginning of what came to be a defining mark of Methodism—pursuing not only spiritual disciplines aimed at deepening one's faith and love for God, but also acts of mercy and compassion, serving as Christ's hands among the poor and those in need of care. The group viewed these two activities as two sides of the same coin, loving God and loving neighbor. Each was an integral part of the other and served as a complement to it. We'll consider in more detail the social ministry of Methodists in Chapter 5.

A Faith Uniting Head and Heart

One of the defining marks of Wesley's own faith and of the eighteenth-century Methodist revival was that it involved not only the emotions but also the intellect—the head as well as the heart. This fact should not surprise us, as the leader of the revival was, after all, a faculty member of Oxford University. When I first joined The United Methodist Church as a nineteen-year-old college student, I was drawn to the fact that this was a church where I was encouraged to think. It was okay to have questions and doubts. I didn't have to "check my brain at the door."

It was also a church that accepted and encouraged emotion. At the age of fourteen, I came to faith in Christ in a wonderful Pentecostal church. I was deeply affected by the passionate faith, the love for the Scriptures, and the wonderful fellowship among Christians in that church. I learned to pray, memorize Scripture, seek a personal relationship with Jesus Christ, and be open to the work of the Holy Spirit. These characteristics and practices in the Pentecostal tradition were also an important part of the eighteenth-century Methodist revival.

Charles Parham, one of the key founders of modern Pentecostalism, had begun his ministry as a Methodist. He attended, for a time, Methodist-related Southwestern College in Winfield, Kansas. But eventually he dropped out of college, believing that education was a hindrance to his ministry. He left the Methodist movement in part believing that Methodists, in their preaching, did not rely enough on direct inspiration by the Holy Spirit. To this day, pastors in most Pentecostal traditions may be ordained with no formal education. We should also add that Pentecostals, like the Methodists before them, went on to found colleges, universities, and seminaries.

A balance between head and heart was what led me in college to The United Methodist Church. As I read about Wesley and the eighteenth-century Methodist revival, I discovered a faith that embraced the emotive elements I valued most in the Pentecostal tradition but that also embraced learning, education, and the intellect as much as I did. Intellectual interest was coupled with a passionate personal faith in Jesus Christ.

I'm reminded of the movie *A River Runs Through It*, based on Norman Maclean's novella of the same name. Among my favorite lines in the movie is when the Presbyterian father describes Methodists as "Baptists who can read." Baptists were known for their evangelical fervor and zeal, while Presbyterians and Episcopalians were known for their emphasis on education and the intellect. The Methodist revival led by Wesley sought to balance intellect and emotion, head and heart.

To religious skeptics, most vocal expressions of Christianity today seem to be anti-intellectual. There is a sense among many nonreligious people I meet that the only way to be a Christian is to sacrifice modern science, to adopt a very narrow view of the world, to interpret the Bible literally and woodenly, and to refrain from asking difficult questions of faith. Yet Wesley, the Oxford fellow and preacher, had a way of holding together a passionate faith and a rigorous intellect. I believe that approach to Christianity holds the greatest promise for reaching an increasingly secular society.

God gave us a brain and a heart. He wants us to use both. Jesus taught us to love God with our "heart and soul" as well as our "mind and strength." This union of emotion and intellect has been a hallmark of Methodism. In America, the same folks who held religious revivals called camp meetings started colleges and universities to educate leaders who would change the world.

I live in Kansas. The first university of any kind in our state was Baker University, founded by the Methodists. The University of Missouri, Kansas City, was the vision of the Methodist Church, and its first classes were held in the Central Methodist Church. Methodists started hundreds of colleges and universities throughout the country, including Duke, Syracuse, Southern Methodist, Emory, Northwestern, the University of Southern California, Boston University, Vanderbilt, and many more.

At the beginning of this chapter I quoted a passage from First Peter that begins, "Therefore prepare your minds for action; discipline yourselves; set all your hope on the grace that Jesus Christ will bring you when he is revealed." I love this passage, because it involves intellect, spiritual discipline, and faith. We are to love God with our minds and with our hearts.

Wesley scholar Henry D. Rack captured this dual emphasis of the Methodist revival when he described Wesley as a "reasonable enthusiast."[12] *Enthusiast* was a derogatory term in the eighteenth century. The word literally means "filled with God." It was used to describe someone who was passionate, even fanatical. Wesley's opponents sought to label him and his followers as fanatics. But Wesley's passion was not that of the fanatics who left reason aside. Wesley was a reasonable enthusiast. A spiritual revival in our time must include both passion and intellect.

At the church I serve, our hope is for every member to be theologically informed, spiritually transformed, and effectively serving God in the world. We want our members to feel capable of addressing the questions, concerns, and doubts raised by their non-Christian friends. We want them, in other words, always to "be ready to make your defense to anyone who demands from you an accounting for the hope that is in you; yet do it with gentleness and reverence" (1 Peter 3:15-16).

A Longing for Holiness

As important as it was to unite head and heart, that wasn't enough for Wesley. He at times felt his own faith to be inadequate. He had a deep desire to do everything for the glory of God. There was, welling up in him, a longing for holiness. That longing was expressed in another passage from 1 Peter: "Like obedient children, do not be conformed to the desires that you formerly had in ignorance. Instead, as he who called you is holy, be holy yourselves in all your conduct; for it is written, 'You shall be holy, for I am holy'" (1 Peter 1:14-16).

At Oxford, the small band of Christians Wesley was mentoring shared his longing for holiness. For Wesley and his friends, holiness included a complete yielding of one's life to God, a desire to become like Christ in heart and actions, acts of compassion for others, and a resolution to live one's life for God's glory. Among the ways Wesley pursued this quest

49

for holiness was rising at four or five o'clock in the morning for private prayer; fasting two days a week until mid-afternoon; and meeting with others to study the Bible and other Christian writings; and to hold each other accountable. Wesley and his friends attended public worship and received the Eucharist weekly. They read and meditated upon Scripture daily. They actively pursued acts of compassion and mercy for the poor, the prisoners, and the elderly, and they sought to achieve lives of simplicity.[13]

This rigorous pursuit of holiness by Wesley and the students he mentored caused others at Oxford to ridicule them calling them "Bible moths" and the "Holy Club." They were labeled "Methodists" for their intentional and methodical approach in pursuing holiness.

Restoration Projects

Wesley and his Oxford Methodists, through the pursuit of the spiritual practices described above, invited the Holy Spirit to change them. They believed humanity is marred by sin. Their hope was to be restored by the Spirit and made into what God intends—human beings who wholly love God and love their neighbors as they love themselves.

According to Wesley, the very meaning of religion is the recovery of God's image in us. Drawing upon the New Testament metaphor of redemption, Wesley taught that Jesus purchases us and the Spirit works to restore us. Spiritual practices such as prayer, worship, receiving the sacraments, journaling, reading the Bible, and serving others are tools the Spirit uses to transform us. Wesley believed that the goal of the Christian life is to be holy as God is holy—to be consumed by love for God and neighbor, to avoid evil and do good always and everywhere, and to pursue the practices that deepen our love for God.

We're All Junkers

One metaphor I've found useful in describing God's work in the life of Christians is that of restoring old cars. I once preached an entire sermon series using this metaphor. I found a 1966 Mustang convertible, in terrible condition, sitting at an area junkyard. We bought the junker and had it towed to the church, where we pushed it onto the chancel in our sanctuary for the four weeks of the sermon series. A church member had a beautifully restored Mustang that we also had brought onto the chancel. (We have a large chancel.) We interviewed people who restore old Mustangs, inviting them to describe the process of restoration. Then we used their words and these two cars to illustrate spiritual restoration.

I remember interviewing the guys who ran the Mustang junkyard in Kansas City. I asked one of them, "What do you see when you look at these dilapidated Mustangs in the salvage yard?" He said, "I don't see them as they are. I see what they could be." What a powerful picture of how God views us. The church is God's salvage yard, and he sees what we could be. Our task is to invite him to restore us. As we do, little by little he strips us down to the bare metal and then begins perfectly restoring us.

If we're willing to pursue the Christian life, if we're willing to say, "Take me, Lord—my heart, my life, my all—and make me what you want me to be," then God, through the Spirit, will restore us. (In the next chapter we'll consider the "means of grace" that aid the Spirit's work of our restoration.)

As the sermon series ended, I discussed the three types of restored cars. Some are called "trailer queens," because they are moved from show to show on trailers and never driven. Others are "Sunday only" cars, driven just on the occasional Sunday when the weather is fair. But to me the best restoration projects are the "daily drivers," driven regularly, often daily. I noted that those calling themselves Christians can be found in each of these three categories, too. I ended the final sermon and worship service by getting into the restored Mustang and driving away, encouraging our members to be "daily drivers" and take their faith to the streets.

Where are you in the restoration process? Is your faith that of a "daily driver"?

There are times when I feel I have lost some of my passion and longing to be holy as God is holy, when I am content to be only partially restored, when my desire to do all for the glory of God wanes. Does that ever happen with you?

An interesting thing happens to cars that have been restored. After ten or fifteen years they start to rust again. They get chips and dings and dents. The paint begins to fade, and the carpet begins to wear. You can't restore a car once and assume it's good for life. The restoration job is ongoing. Sometimes, when you've been a Christian for years and years, you become comfortable, content, satisfied, and you lose your passion to be fully restored. Is your restoration job looking a bit worn? Perhaps it's time for you to place your life in God's hands once again, to invite the Holy Spirit to begin a fresh restoration, and to reclaim some of the spiritual practices you once pursued.

What to See in Oxford

Oxford is an essential stop for anyone visiting England to retrace Wesley's footsteps. Located 140 miles from Epworth and 60 miles from London, it is a delightful college town, founded in the tenth century near the junction of the Cherwell and Thames Rivers and named for the site of a ford where oxen crossed.

These days Oxford has a population of more than 150,000 people, and it's often teeming with visitors. You can reach it from London, on trains that leave Paddington Station every fifteen minutes. It takes about an hour to get there. You won't need a car while in Oxford; in fact, it's better not to have one, since parking is a bit of a challenge.

Oxford   ©*iStock.com/andrearoad*

The city looks much the same as it did in Wesley's day, with buildings dating back to the 1200s. Harry Potter fans will feel they've set foot on a film set, because many of the exteriors were filmed at Oxford. C. S. Lewis and J. R. R. Tolkien fans can stop and have a pint in the Eagle and Child, the pub where those two authors and their friends would meet. I find walking the streets around the university campus to be a magical experience. It leaves me wanting to forsake my life in America to indulge in a life of study and academia.

If you want to experience the Wesley sites chronologically, start with Christ Church, the college Wesley attended while at Oxford. Plan to take the guided tour, which takes about an hour. For schedules, cost, and other information, visit the Christ Church website: www.chch.ox.ac.uk/visiting/behind-the-scenes. You'll also find good photos of Christ Church on the website.

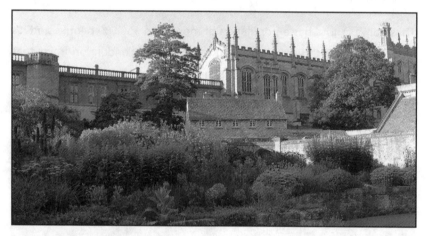

Christ Church, Oxford

Next you'll want to visit Lincoln College, where Wesley was a fellow. (This also was the college of Dr. Seuss!) You can visit the Wesley Room on the second floor, overlooking the quad. The room is decorated with furnishings from Wesley's era and with books that might have been in his library. Admission to visit the Wesley Room is by written request, and there is a nominal fee (www.methodistheritage.org.uk/lincolncollege.htm).

Wesley's Room at Lincoln College

Though this may not have been Wesley's actual room, it is designed to help you imagine Wesley's daily life and the small-group meetings that led to the "first rise of Methodism," with Wesley and his group of altogether Christians. You can easily picture John, Charles, William Morgan, and Bob Kirkham meeting there to pray and encourage one another in the Christian life. As I sat in this room, I was also reminded of the power of Christian mentors, particularly in a university setting. Whether you are a college professor, a schoolteacher, a confirmation mentor, or a Bible study leader for youth or young adults, this kind of investment in students can have profound results.

There's far more to do in Oxford, but you'll definitely want to visit St. Mary's Church. Unlike Christ Church, this is not a college but the University Church of Oxford. It was in this beautiful church that Wesley managed to alienate faculty and students on two occasions: in 1741, when he preached one of his most famous sermons, "The Almost Christian"; and in 1744, when he preached a sermon titled "Scriptural Christianity." He knew this latter sermon might be the last he would be allowed to preach at his beloved Oxford, because he expected to offend the faculty and students. Wesley was right: he was never invited back to preach there.

Interior, St. Mary's Church

Be sure to print off copies of Wesley's sermons "The Almost Christian" and "Scriptural Christianity" before you go to St. Mary's Church. Then read the sermons as you sit in the church, imagining how they would have been received by the students and faculty when Wesley delivered the sermons (www.umcmission.org/Find-Resources/John-Wesley-Sermons/Title-Index).

3.
A Crisis of Faith
Georgia and Aldersgate

For what does the scripture say? "Abraham believed God, and it was reckoned to him as righteousness." Now to one who works, wages are not reckoned as a gift but as something due. But to one who without works trusts him who justifies the ungodly, such faith is reckoned as righteousness. . . . Therefore, since we are justified by faith, we have peace with God through our Lord Jesus Christ, through whom we have obtained access to this grace in which we stand.

(Romans 4:3-5; 5:1-2a)

3.

A Crisis of Faith

Georgia and Aldersgate

In the previous chapter we left John Wesley at Oxford, where he spent the better part of his life from the ages of seventeen to thirty-two. During this time Wesley completed his education, was ordained, and was elected a fellow of Lincoln College, where he taught or tutored Greek Testament. He served for a short time back in Epworth as his father's curate at St. Andrew's, then returned to Oxford, intending to commit his life to the work of educating and mentoring students. More than this, he intended to be an altogether Christian. He hoped to glorify God in everything he did, to be holy in his thoughts, words, and deeds.

The challenge for many Christians in pursuit of the Christian spiritual life, a life of holiness without which, the writer of Hebrews says, "no one can see God," is balancing the quest for holiness with the trust and confidence in God's grace by which we are saved. In other words, when we are focused on our pursuit of holiness, we may find the goal elusive and may never be certain we've done enough to see or please God. As I read Wesley in the period from 1724 to 1738, and intermittently throughout the following decades, he seemed to have struggled with this tendency. This could lead to an ever stricter, more ascetic faith. Or it might lead to an obsessive or compulsive focus on doing good works, or pursuing spiritual disciplines.

I think of the Apostle Paul who, prior to his Christian conversion, had been "zealous for the law,"[1] working to experience God's acceptance but never feeling he had done quite enough. It was only when he had an encounter with Jesus Christ and came to apprehend, accept, and then articulate the truth of salvation by grace through faith that Paul was set free from his desperate attempt to win God's favor. As he notes in Galatians 2:16, "A person is justified not by the works of the law but through faith in Jesus Christ. And we have come to believe in Christ Jesus, so that we might be justified by faith in Christ, and not by doing the works of the law, because no one will be justified by the works of the law." Paul became the greatest evangelist of the first-century church, but only after he finally accepted God's grace through Jesus Christ.

Though he was a Christian and a monk, Martin Luther shared this same struggle that Paul had known. Luther sought to please God, yet the harder he tried the more elusive God's acceptance and favor seemed to be. Luther wrote, "When I was a monk, I wearied myself greatly for almost fifteen years with the daily sacrifice, tortured myself with fastings, vigils, prayers, and other very rigorous works. I earnestly thought to acquire righteousness by my works, nor did I think it possible I should ever forget this life."[2] Luther experienced deep and terrifying spiritual struggles he called *Anfechtungens*, a German word sometimes translated as "trials" or "spiritual crises" and sometimes described by the phrase "dark nights of the soul." In the midst of one of these crisis periods, Luther was driven to reconsider Paul's own testimony in Romans 1:17 about the righteousness of God that is ours by faith. Suddenly Luther "got it" and began to trust God's righteousness and acceptance. Luther described what he felt in that moment: "Then I felt as if I had been completely reborn and had entered Paradise through widely opened doors."[3] Like Paul's, Luther's "conversion" would have a profound impact upon the world.

At times at Oxford, Wesley seemed to be pursuing holiness and righteousness as Luther and Paul had done before him, through his own rigorous actions. He awakened early every morning to pray. He fasted two days a week. He studied the Bible each day. He received the Eucharist weekly and sometimes daily. He regularly visited prisoners, the sick, and the elderly. He refused to cut his hair and instead gave poor people the money he would have paid to a barber.

These efforts were all laudable. When balanced with an assurance of faith and a confidence in the grace of God, they could be signs of a healthy and serious Christian life. In Wesley's head he knew salvation was purely a gift, but often in his heart he seemed to be seeking to win God's acceptance. Wesley's struggle ultimately led to a crisis in his faith similar to Martin Luther's two hundred years before.

Wesley noted that he had "been charged with being too strict . . . with carrying things too far in religion and laying burdens on myself, if not on others, which were neither necessary nor possible to be borne."[4] Though Wesley dismissed the charge, there was truth to it. In the Christian life there is a fine line between a passionate pursuit of holy living and an unhealthy legalism focused on rules and guilt. I wonder if you've ever experienced this. Have you sensed that you can never do enough to win God's favor and be acceptable to him? Have you tried harder and harder, doing more and more to earn his love?

In my congregation, I've seen this tendency most often in people who volunteer for jobs that carry more responsibility than they can or should take on. Then they pursue the jobs at such a frantic pace that no one can keep up with them or meet their expectations, not even the staff. At times they inadvertently drive others away, which may cause them to work even harder to prove to God and others that they are okay. When others don't provide the affirmation they are desperately seeking from God, they become disillusioned, hurt, or angry, and often they leave the church.

It was Wesley's quest to please God and be found holy in God's sight that I believe may have motivated him to leave Oxford and journey as a missionary to the New World.

Journey to America: The Power of the Storm

In 1732, the British established their first new colony in America in five decades. The colony was named Georgia in honor of King George II. James Oglethorpe, a member of Parliament and a social reformer, was both the visionary behind the new colony and its *de facto* leader. He arrived there in 1733 and founded the city of Savannah, then returned to England in 1735 to recruit others and gain additional support for the new colony. There was need for a handful of clergy to serve the community and spread the gospel to the native inhabitants of Georgia. The Oxford Methodists were considered to be just the kind of pastors who might thrive in Georgia.

John Wesley convinced his brother Charles to join him on the mission, along with two of their friends. John hoped to convert the natives and be in ministry with the colonists, but there was something more that seems to have motivated Wesley. Interestingly, Wesley himself noted in his journal that his chief aim in going to America was to save his own soul.[5] Wesley scholar Richard Heitzenrater notes that Wesley had never been on a ship before boarding one for America and that he had "feared the sea from his youth."[6] The journey would require just over three months at sea. I wonder if, subconsciously, Wesley believed that risking life and limb on a terrifying journey to convert the natives would surely prove the seriousness of his faith and his desire to live a holy life. In a sense he was literally fulfilling the words of Paul to the Philippians to work out their salvation "with fear and trembling" (Philippians 2:12).

And so John Wesley, the man who feared the sea, boarded a ship called the *Simmonds* on October 14, 1735. During the three-month journey, the ship encountered terrible storms, and Wesley was terrified that he would die. The storms would shake Wesley to his core and lead him to question his faith.

It's interesting how God works in the storms of life. I'm not suggesting God sends them, though there are a few examples of that in Scripture, but if we're paying attention we certainly can see that God *uses* them and *works through* them. Storms often play a part in great revivals of faith. Noah, Jonah, Peter, and Paul all had profound encounters with God in the midst of storms. Martin Luther, mentioned earlier in this chapter, left his law studies to become a monk because of an experience in a storm. And storms in the Atlantic, during which the terrified Wesley thought he was dying, prepared him for his own Damascus Road experience.

In my own life, the storms have not always been literal, but they have been just as terrifying. When they struck and seemed to blow my life off course, they led eventually to the place where I am today. Storms shaped me, changed me, and pushed me toward new places and new people. When I was a boy, my parents divorced. This was a storm in which, as a twelve-year-old, I thought my world had ended. But through that move I came to faith in Christ and met the girl who would one day become my wife. When as a teen my alcoholic stepfather plunged our home life into constant turmoil, I heard a call to become a pastor. When my best friend died in an accident and I nearly lost my faith, I began searching for answers and ended up a United Methodist. The tragedies and challenges we call the storms of life do not have to destroy us; placed in God's hands, they become part of our defining story and open the door to new possibilities.

For Wesley, the Atlantic storms demonstrated the inadequacy of his cerebral and often works-oriented faith. On January 25, 1736, he recorded in his journal the climax of these storms at sea: the mainsail was in tatters, waves washed over the ship, and the water "poured in between the decks, as if the great deep had already swallowed us up."[7] He observed that the English passengers were screaming in terror, as he was, but a group of German Moravians calmly sang a psalm. This encounter with the Moravian Christians affected Wesley deeply, leading him to focus on the inner assurance of faith that he longed for but did not yet have. In that storm, seeds were planted that would be watered over the next two years and would finally blossom one evening in May 1738, on a London street called Aldersgate. More on that evening in the next chapter.

How *Not* to Win Friends and Influence People

When Wesley arrived in Georgia, he recognized that his faith had shortcomings, but he was still determined to pursue a rigorous path of holiness. He started by confiscating and destroying all the rum on board, which had been sent so the passengers could celebrate their arrival in the New World—not a great way to win friends and influence people, especially since some of the passengers were headed for Savannah, where he would serve as their pastor![8]

On reaching Savannah, Wesley began his ministry more passionate than ever about pursuing holiness. His preaching drew people to him, and some began to follow his methodical approach to the Christian life, so that later he described his ministry in Georgia as the "second rise of Methodism."

While some embraced and pursued the vision of Christian life that Wesley advocated, for others it was simply too much. For instance, John held five a.m. prayer services each day, which in itself was not a problem. The problem came when he declared that only those attending the early-morning service could receive the Eucharist![9] Wesley also encouraged fasting until tea time, not just on Fridays but also on Wednesdays, as was practiced at times in the early church.[10]

It was this kind of rigid and more rigorous approach to faith that began to alienate some among his flock. At one point Wesley reported that a parishioner told him, "I like nothing you do. . . . Indeed there is neither man nor woman in the town who minds a word you say. And so you may preach long enough; but nobody will come to hear you."[11]

At times a pursuit of holiness can lead Christians, as it seems to have done at times with Wesley, to Pharisaic tendencies, including a faith where rules dominate and others are judged harshly. I consider myself a recovering Pharisee. It happens to many Christians I know. It's what people outside the church often say about Christians today: rather than being known for our love, we're known for our judgmentalism. When we have an unbalanced faith, focused on the pursuit of holiness without a corresponding experience of grace, we can easily become Pharisees. I think of a man I know who believes he is a devout and mature Christian. Yet he's quick to make harsh comments on others' Facebook pages or their blogs. He sees himself as a champion of orthodoxy, and though he upholds Christian doctrine, he lacks the fruit of the Spirit: "love, joy, peace, patience, kindness, generosity, faithfulness, gentleness, and self-control" (Galatians 5:22-23). Like most of us, he's blind to his own shortcomings and cannot see that his words actually push people from Christ.

Sometimes those who struggle with legalistic or judgmental tendencies haven't yet experienced God's grace, or have experienced it but only in the distant past. It's hard to treat others with grace when we haven't experienced or been immersed in grace ourselves. Grace is a gift. It is not deserved. It is a reflection not of the recipient's goodness but of the giver's generosity. It is surprising, overwhelming, and amazing. When we truly understand the nature of grace, it fills our hearts in a way that John Wesley did not yet grasp.

The Crisis Comes to a Head

By the summer of 1736, Wesley was meeting regularly with small groups in Savannah. Group members were typically people in their late teens or early twenties who were serious about growing in their faith. They would pray, read Scripture, discuss it, and then listen as Wesley read from William Law or another writer on the Christian life. After further discussion they would pray once more. The meetings were patterned after Wesley's meetings at Oxford and after those held by the Moravians in Savannah, with whom Wesley remained in contact.

Among the people who came to Wesley's meetings was a pretty young woman named Sophia Hopkey. She was seventeen or eighteen, the age when most women married. Sophia, along with her uncle and guardian Thomas Causton, wanted to find a suitable mate for her. John, with his long hair, attractive features, and godly and charismatic personality, seemed a perfect match, though at the time he was thirty-two.

Sophia was drawn to Wesley, and he to her. In his journals he described the struggle with his attraction to Sophia, which seems to have intertwined romance and spirituality. Wesley, perhaps drawing upon the Apostle Paul's admonition in 1 Corinthians 7 that it may be better not to marry, at times seemed committed to celibacy. He thought that the two of them might be able to continue sharing a deep, spiritual, platonic yet subtly romantic relationship.

But Sophia wanted a husband, and so, while continuing her relationship with Wesley, she secretly accepted the advances of a man named William Williamson and became engaged to him. When John found out, he was heartbroken, both by the engagement itself and by the fact that she had been accepting Williamson's advances while meeting with Wesley for spiritual encouragement. That heartbreak led to a storm far greater than those at sea, and, like those storms, it ultimately contributed to the great revival Wesley would lead.

Sophia and Williamson were hastily married, and afterward John found it difficult to be her pastor without acting on the hurt he felt. At one point he barred her from receiving communion. She came forward anyway, and he refused her in front of the congregation. His refusal led to charges being filed against Wesley in court by Sophia and her husband, claiming defamation of character. The court proceedings, which sound like a soap opera, continued for several months, with an increasing number of parishioners growing weary of their pastor. In December of that year, Wesley left by night for Charleston, where he boarded a ship back to England.

Wesley's dreams for the mission to America were dashed. His heart, pride, and spirit were broken. He returned to England a complete failure.

Praising God for the Storms

Wesley didn't know it at the time, but the rejection he had suffered, the spiritual and pastoral disasters he had experienced, and the sense of utter failure would have an incalculable impact upon his world and ours. His fear in the face of death during the storms at sea caused him to seek more than simply knowing the truth and doing all he could to be holy. His failure in America led him finally to be seized by a saving grace, received solely by faith. All these experiences played an important role in preparing Wesley for the great work God would do through him in the eighteenth-century evangelical revival.

Our failures, placed in God's hands, often lead to our greatest successes. Our most painful experiences become our defining moments by the grace of God, provided that we learn from them. This is what Paul was teaching in Romans 8:28: "We know that all things work together for good for those who love God, who are called according to his purpose."

The challenge for many of us is that we spend so much time blaming others for our failures and expressing disappointment in God that we miss an opportunity to be teachable and to learn from the experience. God takes the dark moments, the failures and rejections in our lives, and uses them for our good—if we allow it, if we humble ourselves and consider whether there is anything in us that needs to be changed. (The Bible calls this process repentance—to have a change of heart that results in a change in our thinking and ultimately a change in behavior.)

I've known people who reached such a point when the world was crashing down around them, as Wesley's was, and instead of asking what they might need to change, they justified themselves and pointed a finger at everyone else. But there is great power in honestly assessing how we ended up where we are and inviting God to teach us, shape us, and forgive us. In this teachable position, humbled before God, we are often surprised by what happens next.

Recently I spoke with a member of the church I serve who had lost his job a couple of years before. He said, "Four times in my career there were critical moments when things did not go as I had planned. I'm old enough to look back and say, 'Each time, what ultimately happened in the aftermath was better than what I had planned.'"

Wesley was humbled and broken when he came back to England. He seemed to have become more teachable. All his best attributes were still there, but his failure eventually led to a profound spiritual awakening and to the passion and conviction that provided the impetus for the Methodist revival.

This is what James was referring to, I think, when he wrote, "My brothers and sisters, whenever you face trials of any kind, consider it nothing but joy, because you know that the testing of your faith produces endurance; and let endurance have its full effect, so that you may be mature and complete, lacking in nothing" (James 1:2-4).

I wonder if you've given your failures and disappointments to God, then invited God to teach you through them. Have you been relentless in seeking to grow as a result of them, and have you trusted God to bring good from them? This is far harder than remaining resentful and blaming others, even when there are others we can rightly blame. As Wesley learned, healing and grace and new beginnings come when we let go of the right to be angry.

Accepting God's Acceptance

When Wesley returned to England, in the depths of despair, he recalled the faith of the German Moravians and sought out a Moravian missionary named Peter Boehler, who was preparing to leave for Georgia. Wesley had planned to stop preaching until he regained his faith, but Boehler's response changed his mind. Boehler's words are known by nearly every Methodist preacher (though most assume Wesley said them): "Preach faith *till* you have it, and then, *because* you have it, you *will* preach faith."[12] Following Boehler's advice, Wesley went about preaching about salvation by faith alone. His words touched some, led others to ban him from preaching in their churches again, and laid the foundation for his own experience of grace.

On May 24, 1738, Wesley went to a religious society that met in a house on Aldersgate Street in London. Religious society meetings typically were small groups of people who came together to confess their sins to one another, pray together, hold each other accountable, and, in the words of Hebrews, "provoke one another to love and good deeds" (Hebrews 10:24).

Scholars debate the precise meaning of the event that took place that night. At the very least, Wesley experienced grace in a way he had never felt before. This man who was trying so hard to prove himself to God (or to himself) discovered that God offered freely what Wesley had worked so hard to attain. This is how he described the experience in his journal:

In the evening I went very unwillingly to a society in Aldersgate Street, where one was reading Luther's Preface to the Epistle to the Romans. About a quarter before nine, while he was describing the change which God works in the heart through faith in Christ, I felt my heart strangely warmed. I felt I did trust in Christ, Christ alone for salvation; and an assurance was given me that he had taken away *my* sins, even *mine*, and saved *me* from the law of sin and death. I began to pray with all my might for those who had in a more especial manner despitefully used me and persecuted me. I then testified openly to all there what I now first felt in my heart.[13]

Wesley was so moved by his experience of grace that at times he suggested he hadn't even been a Christian before that night on Aldersgate Street. Later he recognized that in fact he had been a Christian before that night. But in that moment of complete trust, he had experienced in a new way the love of God and the deliverance and salvation that come only by faith. To the degree that at times he wrestled with doing "enough" to please God, on that night he knew the undeserved, unearned love of God. He knew it not only with his head, but with his heart as well.

Rules-based faith imagines a God who is never satisfied. This type of faith may be based on guilt, fear, or doubt about doing enough to please God. Wesley's Aldersgate experience pointed to one of the essential truths of the gospel: that out of his great love for us, God has taken the initiative to save and deliver us. Our lives are lived in grateful response.

I once knew a young woman whose father was never satisfied with her. He never said he loved her or was proud of her. She pushed herself in school, but when her report card showed five A's and a B, he asked why she hadn't received straight A's. When she graduated salutatorian, he said if she had just tried a little harder she could have been the valedictorian. She drove herself to win her father's approval, but he always withheld it.

Carrying Rocks

I used a metaphor in a series of sermons I preached several years ago that many found helpful. I had a backpack on the chancel and a pile of rocks next to it. In one sermon I noted that the rocks represented hurts and painful experiences others have inflicted upon us that we must forgive. In another sermon I likened the rocks to the sins we've committed against others, for which we haven't yet asked for or received forgiveness. In still another message I likened the rocks to the guilt we experience when we've sinned against God.

Finally I placed the rocks one by one in the pack, then hoisted it up onto my back. It contained nearly fifty pounds of rocks. I strained under their weight but kept preaching, talking about what it's like to carry around hurt, bitterness, and resentment toward others; or feelings of guilt and anxiety when we've hurt others but haven't yet asked forgiveness; or guilt when we're uncertain that God has forgiven us.

I suggested that in each case, our condition represents a burden we carry with us. It slows us down in all we do. We're unable to leap, dance, or play. Eventually it takes a physical toll on us. The orthopedic surgeons in our congregation winced as they watched me move around the chancel, preaching with a heavy load on my back.

Then I described the biblical concept of grace: the grace we extend to those who have hurt us, the grace we seek from others when we confess and repent, and the grace we accept from God. When I finished, I took off the backpack and let it drop to the floor with a thud. I was amazed at how I felt once the backpack was removed. I felt light. I felt free. In that moment I thought I could fly.

I suspect Wesley knew that feeling. After all the years of struggle and hardship, he dropped the burden one night in May of 1738 and accepted God's grace. After that night, grace became a defining attribute of his life and a continuing theme in his preaching and theology.

For many people, this young woman's relationship with her father characterizes their relationship with God. Yet God is not like that earthly father. God knows our shortcomings yet loves us still.

I get a glimpse of God's love for us in my relationship with my daughters. I love both of them dearly and would do anything for them.

As they were growing up, from time to time they would occasionally do things that disappointed me. When they did, I was ready to forgive even before they were ready to ask. Then, as now, I savor the time I get to spend with them. I want to bless them. I love them with all my heart. And yet God's love for us, and his grace toward us, is infinitely greater.

Wesley encountered that love after a season of discouragement. He had pursued a rigorous life of service to Christ, yet lacked assurance of his salvation and God's grace. But in that moment on Aldersgate Street, he experienced the grace of God that comes to us through Jesus Christ and the peace that Paul described in Romans:

> Since we are justified by faith, we have peace with God through our Lord Jesus Christ, through whom we have obtained access to this grace in which we stand. (Romans 5:1-2a)

Twentieth-century existentialist theologian Paul Tillich expressed so well the spiritual struggle Wesley (and Paul and Luther and perhaps you) experienced and the profound change in perspective that he gained that night at Aldersgate:

> It strikes us when, year after year, the longed-for perfection of life does not appear, when the old compulsions reign within us as they have for decades, when despair destroys all joy and courage. Sometimes at that moment a wave of light breaks into our darkness, and it is as though a voice were saying: "You are accepted. *You are accepted*, accepted by that which is greater than you. . . . Do not try to do anything now; perhaps later you will do much. Do not seek for anything; do not perform anything; do not intend anything. *Simply accept the fact that you are accepted!*" If that happens to us, we experience grace.

After such an experience we may not be better than before, and we may not believe more than before. But everything is transformed. In that moment, grace conquers sin, and reconciliation bridges the gulf of estrangement.[14]

Wesley had been a Christian his whole life. Could his Aldersgate experience be called a conversion? Yes, in the sense that on that night he experienced something he had not felt in quite the same way before. He accepted God's acceptance. His faith moved from his head to his heart.

I remember sitting in a nursing home with a wonderful Methodist woman named Helen. She was in her 80s and was recuperating from a fall. As we visited, she told me her faith story. She had been a Methodist her entire life. She had served in every leadership position in the church. She was a tremendous volunteer. Even then, as she was recuperating, she was anxious to come back to church. As I prepared to pray with her she said, "Can I tell you something I've been afraid to tell anyone else?" I said, "Sure, Helen, what is it?" She told me, "You speak of Christ in such a personal way. You talk with him, you trust him, you speak as though he were your daily companion. I've never known what that was like. I believe in him. And I've sought to serve him. I read my Bible. I pray. But I've never felt his presence, or the sense that he loved me."

I told Helen that it was clear to me she was God's child and that she had faithfully followed Christ her whole life. I said, "I want you to remember, Helen, that every moment you are alive, Christ is here by your side. I came here simply to remind you of this. And Helen, he does love you. You are his child, his beloved. Your task is to trust that this is so."

I went on to say, "I want you to think of the moment in your life when you felt most loved by another—maybe your father or mother when you were a little girl. That is a glimpse of the love Christ has for you. Helen, that's how I think about him. The Bible tells me that he loves me deeply, and I trust that it's so. And then I rest in that love. I talk with him daily,

I thank him a lot, and I listen for him throughout the day in people like you, in my experiences, and chiefly in the Scriptures I read." Then I invited Helen to pray with me these words: "Lord, I believe that you love me. I love you too. I offer all that I am and all that I have to you. Help me to trust, like a little child, that you are always by my side. And help me to live for you and honor you, in all that I do." No one had ever invited Helen to do something as simple and powerful as placing her life in God's hands and personally trusting God's love. Helen had been a Christian her whole life, but in that moment she trusted in the unfailing love of God made known to us in Jesus Christ. That's how I view Wesley's experience on Aldersgate Street.

Though Wesley would reflect upon that experience in different ways throughout his life, it always imparted passion to his love of God and zeal to his preaching of salvation by grace through faith.

Here's the key to the life God intends for us: not that we work as servants with salvation as our wage, but that we live in relationship with God as children to a Father who has already said, "I accept you! I accept you! You are accepted!" Have you accepted God's acceptance of you? The simple act of trust changed Wesley's life, and it could change yours, too.

What to See in Georgia
and at Aldersgate Street in London

If you're ever visiting Savannah, Georgia, stop by Reynolds Square, where you can see a statue of John Wesley that marks his brief ministry in America. Wesley preached near this spot in a hut that served as both church and courthouse. His parsonage was just across the street.

If you have time, visit Fort Pulaski National Monument on Cockspur Island along the Georgia coast. It was here that Wesley disembarked the *Simmonds* after a stormy Atlantic crossing and conducted a service of thanksgiving, his first in the New World. A monument marks the event.

John Wesley monument, Fort Pulaski ©Deborah Crane

Flame sculpture at Aldersgate Street

In London, you'll want to stop and visit Aldersgate Street, where Wesley had his experience of grace. The house no longer exists, and there is some debate as to precisely where it was. Today the Museum of London sits atop what some consider to be the location. A large bronze sculpture, something like a flame, sits outside the main entrance to the museum and includes Wesley's account of that night in May of 1738 when his heart was strangely warmed. Just a few paces away is Postman's Park, whose fence is marked by a sign commemorating the "evangelical conversion" of John Wesley.

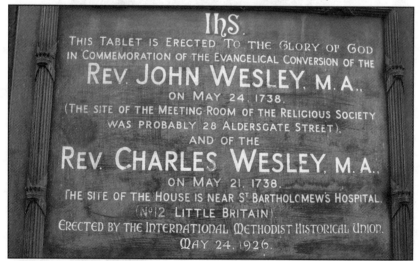

Plaque at Postman's Park

4.
The Necessity of Grace
Bristol

For by grace you have been saved through faith, and this is not your own doing; it is the gift of God—not the result of works, so that no one may boast. For we are what he has made us, created in Christ Jesus for good works, which God prepared beforehand to be our way of life.

(Ephesians 2:8-10)

4.

The Necessity of Grace
Bristol

What Is Grace?

John Wesley drew from this text in Ephesians no fewer than forty times in his preaching. He went back to it again and again. The message that salvation was a gift, accepted and not earned, was something he had always known in his head; but with the help of Peter Boehler and the Moravians, leading to his experience on Aldersgate Street, he finally trusted it in his heart.

I memorized the passage years ago, and I encourage you to do the same. It may have been the Apostle Paul's most important contribution to the Christian faith. Its power could only be fully appreciated by someone such as Wesley who had worked so hard to win God's approval.

Grace is a fundamental concept in the Christian faith, and it was pivotal for Wesley's understanding of the gospel. The Greek word translated as "grace" in the New Testament is *charis*. It appears 148 times in the New Testament. Like its English equivalent, *charis* can have many meanings: someone is said to move with grace, to act gracefully, to have style and grace. But that's not the sense in which Paul uses the word in Ephesians.

Charis, as Paul uses it, is an act of kindness, an expression of selfless love that is completely undeserved and is given without any expectation of repayment. We are never more like God than when we are giving selflessly to others. Because God created us to live in this way, we seldom feel more alive and joyful than when we are serving, blessing, and helping someone else. That is *charis*. It is grace.

If you study Paul's use of the word *charis* in the New Testament, you'll discover that, for him, grace has two distinct meanings, and both are critical for understanding Wesley's theology. The first meaning is grace as *a quality of God's character whereby God loves, blesses, and forgives humanity despite our sin*. The second meaning is grace as *God's active work by the Spirit to draw us to God and to restore us to what God created us to be*. Let's consider, in turn, each of these understandings of grace.

Grace as a Quality of God's Character

Some people picture God as an angry judge or judgmental parent who can never be satisfied, one who sees our sins and shortcomings and is constantly disappointed with us. But Jesus painted a very different series of pictures. God is a shepherd who searches for lost sheep. God is a father who runs to meet his prodigal child. God is a friend of drunkards, prostitutes, and every other kind of sinner. God is gracious and merciful. God feels compassion and great love for God's children.

Many of us didn't grow up seeing God in this way. Our faith focused instead on guilt and shame, reinforced every weekend at church when we heard one more sermon on our sinfulness and God's wrath. Yes, we are sinners, but the dominant message of the gospel is not that we sin but that Jesus saves. His message was not guilt-laden but grace-laden. When Jesus spoke harshly to sinners, it was to religious leaders whose legalistic and judgmental faith was pushing others away from God. Jesus was chastised by the religious leaders of his day for being a friend of sinners.

It was grace that led God to create all things. It is grace that leads God to show mercy to the human race. It is grace that leads God to sustain life on our planet. We recognize this when we describe life as a gift. Our existence is an act of God's generosity and love. Every good thing in our lives is, in an ultimate sense, a reflection of God's grace. We rightly respond to that grace with worship, praise, and a heart and life filled with gratitude.

Grace as God's Active Work on Us

The second sense of grace in Paul's letters is that of God's active influence by the Spirit in our lives. Through this grace, God draws us closer in, and when we accept it, God forgives us and justifies our faith. This same grace is constantly at work in our lives to sanctify us, to form and shape us, and to restore us to become the people God created humanity to be.

Though we don't dwell on sin, we must be aware of it. In the New Testament, the Greek word most often translated as "sin" is *hamartia*. In the Old Testament, the Hebrew word often translated as "sin" is some variation of *chata*. (Note, however, that Hebrew has a number of words that are also translated as "sin.") Both *hamartia* and *chata* originally had the sense of missing the mark or straying from the path. In the Bible, sin is the act of walking away from God's way, but it also is a force at work in us that leads us from God's way.

I once had a car whose front end was out of alignment. If I let go of the steering wheel while traveling down the highway, the car would veer to the right and run off the road. Driving the car, I constantly felt the pull of the wheel, and I would need to countersteer constantly to keep the car on the road. This is the effect of the force or influence we call sin. Surely you've felt it. Paul described it this way in Romans 7:19-20: "I do not do the good I want, but the evil I do not want is what I do. Now if I do what I do not want, it is no longer I that do it, but sin that dwells within me."

Sin ruins things. The story of Adam and Eve is an archetypal story reminding us that turning from God's path (sinning) destroys paradise. It brings pain and shame and death. But grace, in the second sense Paul wrote about, is God's influence aimed at delivering us from sin, bringing us to God, and ultimately repairing our "front end" so that we are perfected and restored and we operate as God intended when God created human beings.

Prevenient, Justifying, and Sanctifying Grace

Wesley spoke about at least three forms of grace. The first is *prevenient grace*, sometimes called preventing grace, which is God's work in us before we even know to reach out to God. It is God's influence in our lives before we come to faith—wooing us, beckoning us, drawing us to God. Prevenient grace is not irresistible. It does not overrun our free will. It is often only in hindsight that we can see this form of grace at work in our lives.

In my own life, I can look back and see people God used to help me and teach me long before I chose to accept Christ. When I was a little boy, my Roman Catholic grandmother taught me to pray, took me to mass, and gave our family the Bible I would one day open and read to find Christ. When I was fourteen, a man named Harold Thorson was visiting door-to-door in my neighborhood, inviting people to church. My parents were at work, so I was the one who spoke to him. There was something about his invitation that I couldn't shake, and that Sunday I went to church for the first time in years. I could give many other examples of God reaching out to me, and working in me, before I knew to reach out to him. I suspect that you have examples of your own.

A second form of grace is *justifying grace*. Wesley taught that we experience justifying grace when we finally say yes to God, when we learn to trust the Christ who gave his life to redeem, save, and deliver us from sin. This form of grace is God's declaration that we are delivered from sin and death, and at the same time it is God's power working in our hearts to free us from guilt and death and to reconcile, redeem, and make us new. Jesus spoke of being "born again" or born from above. In Wesley's sermon "The New Birth," he talks about the change God works in us when we accept his grace and yield our lives to him: "It is that great change which God works in the soul when he brings it into life: when he raises it from the death of sin to the life of righteousness."[1]

Prevenient grace makes it possible to hear, understand, and respond to God's gift of salvation; justifying grace comes when you say yes to God, yielding your life and experiencing the new birth. Of that new birth, Paul writes, "If anyone is in Christ, there is a new creation: everything old has passed away; see, everything has become new!" (2 Corinthians 5:17). And yet, we are not made perfect when we experience that new birth, which leads us to the third form of grace.

My first grandchild was born as I was writing this book. Her name is Stella. Her very life is a gift, both of God and of her parents. She can do nothing to support herself right now. Every meal eaten, every diaper changed is the work of someone else as an expression of love for her. Her entire life is bathed in grace.

I held Stella shortly after she was born, when she was wrapped in a swaddling blanket. She could not understand or see or imagine what the future would hold. But I began thinking of places I would take her, experiences I would have with her, and dreams I hoped for her. I whispered to her through my tears, "Little one, we are going to have so much fun together in the years ahead!" Only God knows what is in store for Stella, but one thing is clear: being born is just the beginning!

The same is true when we finally accept Christ and are justified: it's just the beginning! From there God has plans for us. God wishes to guide us, shape us, restore us, lead us, and use us across the course of our lives, until that day when our life on earth is completed and we are welcomed into the eternal kingdom. God's work in us after we are born again, helping us mature and grow and become what we were meant to be, is achieved through the Holy Spirit. Wesley spoke of it as God's *sanctifying grace*.

As with the other two forms of grace, we can resist sanctifying grace or cooperate with it. The ultimate goal is that we might be completely sanctified, a word that means to be made holy. Wesley, when pressed, said that sanctification means we finally, fully love God with all our heart, soul, mind, and strength, and we love others as we love ourselves. Paul described the goal of sanctification this way in Ephesians 2:10: "We are what he has made us, created in Christ Jesus for good works, which God prepared beforehand to be our way of life."

It is interesting to see that after Aldersgate, Wesley came back to the idea of holiness and good works. The difference was that now the good works were no longer attempts to prove his love for God or win divine favor, affection, and approval; good works were a way of life and would come more easily. The fruit of the Spirit will lead to good works. We will do them without thinking, and they will become second nature to us. They are expressions of gratitude for a gift already given, not a desperate attempt to gain God's acceptance.

The Means of Grace

As we seek to grow in our faith and open ourselves to the Spirit's sanctifying work, we do so by using what Wesley called the means of grace. These are the ordinary channels by which God's prevenient, justifying, and sanctifying grace come to us. As we practice the means of grace, we hear, experience, and receive God's work in us.

In his sermon "The Means of Grace," Wesley mentioned several of the practices through which God's grace is communicated and conveyed in our lives: prayer, Scripture reading, and partaking of the Lord's Supper. In what became known as the General Rules of the Methodist Societies, he also mentioned public worship, preaching, fasting, and abstinence. In addition to these, there are many other means by which God pours his grace into our lives: serving in mission and ministry with others, reading books on the Christian life, walking in silence through the woods, spending time with a small group of Christians in conversation about faith. Often God's grace comes to me simply by my paying attention to what is happening around me, listening carefully to the stories of others, spending time with my children, or writing in a journal. The key is paying attention, listening to God's Spirit with the ears and the heart.

Ultimately, these practices should lead us to be a little more graceful tomorrow than we were yesterday. If we are more fully surrendered to the Spirit, we should exhibit more of the fruit of the Spirit in our lives next year than we did last year. Likewise, attention to the means of grace should lead us to a greater compassion for others, a deeper desire to care for the poor and the powerless, and a greater commitment to justice.

It's hard for me to see growth in myself, but I can see it in my wife LaVon. She's always been an amazing person. She stole my heart years ago. But when I watch her today caring for our adult children, for our friends, and for me, I see God's sanctifying grace in her life. We must be intentional about the goal of sanctification in our lives. We can use the means of grace to become more like Christ. If we don't, we'll often find that we revert back to the misaligned life we once lived, veering off the path of God.

Wesley saw the sanctifying work of the Spirit as a process, but he also believed that at times it could be imparted by the Spirit in an instant.

Wesley heard accounts of people who had received an instantaneous experience of the Spirit and afterward claimed a desire to love their neighbor and no desire to sin again. Wesley examined these accounts and took the people at their word. Later in his ministry, having observed some of these people no longer acting with perfect love for God or neighbor, he came to believe it was possible to fall out of this state of sanctification.

On a few occasions, I've been overcome with what I felt was the sanctifying work of the Spirit. I wouldn't claim I was completely sanctified in those moments, but by the definition Wesley gave and the testimony he recounted of those who claimed it, I felt I had experienced something similar. I remember when driving once from Kansas City to Dallas, I turned off the radio and spent several hours singing hymns and praying. In the midst of that time I felt overcome with a love of God and neighbor. On that trip to Dallas I was scheduled to stop by and see someone who had said some uncharitable things about me, and I hoped for reconciliation with that person. I was feeling apprehensive about the visit, but in that moment, singing and praying in the car, the apprehension gave way to a feeling of deep love for and a longing to bless that person. The intense feeling lasted for several days, but I continue, years later, to have a love for that individual. I've experienced several similar moments, and virtually all occurred after prayer, worship, Scripture reading, or long walks talking with the Lord.

Wesley's teaching on sanctification is biblically based and powerful. It provides clarity about goals in our walk with Christ and gives us a way of measuring progress toward those goals. I long to love God with all my heart, soul, mind, and strength. I want to become like Christ as I know and love God more. I want his character to rub off on me. I want to surrender to God's will and purposes more fully tomorrow than I did yesterday. I want to love my neighbor as I love myself. I want to speak words that "give grace to those who hear" (Ephesians 4:29). I want to do justice and love kindness. I pray that the fruit of the Spirit might be experienced by those who know me. I want it to be second nature to care for others, build them up, bless them, and show mercy and compassion toward them. These are not realities in my life all the time, but they do reflect my hopes and aspirations.

Watching people in my own congregation, I notice that some age gracefully, while others become less gracious as the years go by. The difference, I think, has a lot to do with whether we're pursuing the means of grace and if we've set our hearts on the goal of sanctification. Where are you in this process of grace?

I know that many Christians (or almost Christians) come to church and say, "You know, I feel better when I go to church. I like the pastor's sermons, the choir moves me, and I really enjoy that." Then they leave, feeling a bit inspired for the week, and go about their business. They come back the next week for another dose of spirituality and good feelings. That's a great place to start a spiritual journey. But at some point we're meant to understand the need for God's grace and accept salvation. We're meant to say, "Here's my life, Lord. I give it to you. I accept your love and grace and your acceptance of me. I'm yours!" And then we're meant to go deeper in our faith, and to become what God created us to be. We're meant to pray, "Please restore me and make me the person you want me to be."

A lot of people get stuck in prevenient grace and never move beyond it. Others accept God's justifying grace; they accept Christ and his saving work but never go on to sanctification. They've been born anew, but they're content to remain infants.

At the Church of the Resurrection, we regularly talk about our journey in Christ and challenge people to know, love, and serve God. We want people to accept the grace of God, then aim to become theologically and biblically informed (to know God), to be spiritually transformed on the journey to sanctification (to love God), and to pursue in daily life those good works that Paul says in Ephesians 4:22 were meant to be our "way of life" (to serve God).

Field Preaching to the Miners in Bristol and Kingswood

After what has sometimes been called Wesley's "evangelical conversion" on Aldersgate Street in London, he became more passionate about calling others to a saving faith. I imagine he was a little bit like a friend of mine who quit smoking. Seeing how much better she felt and knowing how dangerous smoking really is, she became passionate about coaxing, cajoling, and convincing others to stop smoking. It was a great thing to do, but in her newfound passion she alienated some friends who were smokers. That appears to be how Wesley preached following his Aldersgate experience.

As he preached in London at various churches, he at times offended priests and parishioners alike. Many of them refused to invite him back. If at Oxford he had been mocked as a "Methodist" for his disciplined, rigorous, and methodical approach to the Christian life, he now was routinely called an "enthusiast." As mentioned previously, in the eighteenth century this was not a kind word. It literally means "filled with God," but at that time it carried the sense of being a fanatic—someone who was obnoxiously overzealous. By the end of 1738, only five churches in the London area would still have him in their pulpits.

Sympathizers saw him not as fanatical but as passionate and raised up by God. He proclaimed the gospel to a society of polite, lukewarm Christians who in many ways had become inoculated against vital Christianity by years of religious conflict and a lifetime of proper religion that asked nothing more of them than to attend church once in a while and try to be decent human beings. England in the first half of the eighteenth century needed reviving. But people didn't much like hearing that they were "almost Christian."

Once again God used the rejection Wesley experienced to open a new door. That door would be the key to the entire Wesleyan Revival.

In the spring of 1739, Wesley received a note from his twenty-four-year-old friend George Whitefield, a member of the Methodist group Wesley had mentored at Oxford, inviting Wesley to join him in preaching and ministering at Bristol. Bristol was a town of about 50,000 people located 100 miles west of London. It was a major shipping port out of which some 2,000 slave-trading ships routinely traveled first to Africa, trading goods from England in exchange for slaves; then to America, trading slaves for cotton, tobacco, sugar, and other staples; then back to Bristol.[2] On the eastern edge of Bristol was the village of Kingswood, a name that referred to both the village and the coal-mining region surrounding it. Between the shipping trade and coal mining, there were many working poor whose livelihood and place in life kept them from being a part of the established churches.

Whitefield, like Wesley, had had his own conversion experience, and when it came to passion in preaching he surpassed even the thirty-five-year-old Wesley. Whitefield, too, had been banned from preaching in the established churches. In response, he had gone to where the miners were and had begun preaching outdoors. He was not the first to do so—Baptists had preached in Kingswood half a century before—but Whitefield saw amazing results from his outdoor preaching. Wesley came to watch Whitefield preach to the miners on the afternoon of April 1, 1739. That day as many as 30,000 miners and their families listened to Whitefield preach from a small hillside!

In his journal, Wesley famously described his initial reaction to the idea of "field preaching" and his decision to try it himself.

> I could scarce reconcile myself at first to this *strange way* of preaching in the fields . . . having been all my life (till very lately) so tenacious of every point relating to decency and

order that I should have thought the saving of souls *almost a sin* if it had not been done *in a church*. . . . At four in the afternoon I submitted to "be more vile," and proclaimed in the highways the glad tidings of salvation, speaking from a little eminence in a ground adjoining to the city, to about three thousand people.[3]

Three thousand people! Wesley had never preached to so many at one time in all his life. Besides seeing the crowds, Wesley's initial doubt about the idea of preaching outdoors was overcome when he reflected upon the Sermon on the Mount and realized that Jesus did almost all his preaching outdoors.

England was divided into parishes, each parish having a church and a priest responsible for its people. Priests were not to meddle in each other's parishes. But Oxford fellows, nearly all of whom were priests, were not assigned to a particular parish. This included Wesley, who at that time was still a fellow of Lincoln College, Oxford. When priests complained about Wesley's preaching outdoors in their parishes, Wesley reminded them that, as a part of the faculty of Oxford, "the world is my parish."

A few days after preaching for the first time to the miners and their families, Wesley wrote in his journal,

At seven in the morning I preached to about a thousand persons at Bristol, and afterwards to about fifteen hundred on the top of Hanham Mount in Kingswood. I called to them in the words of the evangelical prophet, "Ho! every one that thirsteth, come ye to the waters; come and buy wine and milk without money and without price."[4]

The coal miners in Kingswood were a tough lot. Called colliers, they labored at eighty mining pits in the area, working hard and dying young. Their children were poor and uneducated. At the time Wesley preached, there were no churches in Kingswood. George Whitefield described the tears flowing down the blackened faces of the miners as they listened to the gospel preached at Hanham Mount.

That first month in the Bristol area, Wesley recorded in his journal that 47,500 people came to hear him preach outdoors.[5] Some Christians might be surprised to learn that Wesley didn't issue "altar calls." Altar calls weren't invented until the nineteenth century, when Charles Finney began inviting people to come forward after his revivals to demonstrate their commitment to Christ and to the abolition of slavery. Instead Wesley, after offering Christ to his listeners, invited them to "flee from the wrath to come" and attend a meeting of the religious societies, small groups of people who came together to grow in grace.

Soon those religious societies could not accommodate all the people who wanted to attend. Two of the societies came together to purchase land and, with Wesley's help, erected the world's first Methodist meeting house. It was called "the New Room."[6] The two societies became known as the United Society, and their building still stands in Bristol. Completed in 1739, it became the first headquarters for the Methodist mission.

The Importance of Preaching, Music, and Small Groups

Every night of the week, groups of people would gather at the Methodist mission. These new Christians would sing hymns and listen to John, his brother Charles, or other preachers call them to faith and inspire them to go on toward sanctification. Bristol was where Methodism was organized, and it played a central role in the growth and development of the Methodist movement.

Following the pattern at Bristol, Wesley and the eighteenth-century Methodists went on to build hundreds of preaching houses. Wesley did not intend to start a new denomination; he wanted to renew the established church.

Among Wesley's gifts was organizational thinking. He realized that if he did not organize the new converts and develop a system for helping them grow in faith, they soon would fall away. That is in fact what happened with much of the revival preaching in the eighteenth century, as well as in the nineteenth- and twentieth-century revivals that swept England and America. By contrast, Wesley's organization and design for Methodist societies bore enduring fruit among those who found Christ through their mission.

Wesley's early experience at Oxford laid the foundation for the small groups known as "class meetings" and "bands" that came to characterize Methodist discipleship. In Georgia he had continued this practice, though modified based upon what he observed with the Moravians. The various religious societies in which Wesley had participated included gatherings for preaching as well as smaller bands of people who sought to grow in faith.

Drawing upon all these experiences, Wesley drew up a set of guidelines for the Methodist bands that would form at Bristol. They would begin with singing or prayer. Those present would share with one another "freely and plainly the true state of our souls," including the temptations they had felt and the sins they had committed since they last met.[7] Wesley prepared a set of questions that could be asked at each meeting to facilitate the conversation. Scriptures would be examined and discussed. And the meeting would finally end with group members praying for one another.

This idea of weekly small group meetings was central to the Methodist movement, as was the importance of preaching and singing. These three components are essential to renewal within churches today. We need passionate, biblical *preaching* that is evangelical (inviting hearers to trust in and follow Christ) and relevant (speaking to the head, heart, and hands). Where it is found, congregation members leave church each week inspired and are likely to invite their friends. We need vibrant, passionate *music* as part of vibrant congregations where people encounter God. And we certainly need small groups, which are an essential part of Christian community, accountability, and deeper growth in the Christian life. Preaching, music, and *small groups*—and to these three components, as we'll see in the next chapter, Wesley added missional service to the poor, the sick, the children, and anyone else who needed the care of a Christian community.

Free Grace for All

Wesley would go on from Bristol to devote much of his remaining life to preaching outdoors, then organizing those who responded into Methodist societies that gathered in preaching houses for preaching, singing, and prayer. He encouraged these new Christians to meet in small groups once a week, while continuing to participate in their parish churches for worship and the Eucharist.

All Wesley's activities—his outdoor preaching and his willingness to work relentlessly to teach the gospel—were undergirded by an important theological conviction, one that came to characterize most religious movements that trace their lineage to Wesley: God's grace is available to all.[8] Throughout the history of Christian faith, there have been attempts to interpret certain verses in the Bible that refer to predestination and election of people to receive salvation (see Romans 9) in light of other passages that point to God's love for all people and desire for all to be saved (see 1 Timothy 2:4). Christian theologians Augustine and Pelagius debated this issue in the fifth century. Martin Luther and John Calvin shared somewhat different views on predestination in the sixteenth century. Calvin affirmed double predestination, which asserts that God chose those who would be saved and those who would be damned before any of us was born. The choice was unconditional—that is, God chose the elect and the damned based solely upon divine will, not upon anything that people would do or not do in their lives.

Several decades after the death of Calvin, Jacobus Arminius challenged Calvin's teaching concerning election when he asserted conditional predestination and the foreknowledge of God. That is, God, by grace, gives all of us the ability to choose God (Wesley spoke of this gift as prevenient grace); and God, who is omniscient and stands above time, knew from the foundation of the world who would avail themselves of salvation and who would not. Hence God gives the grace for all to choose, and God knows who will choose, and thus in this sense God, before the foundations of the world, predestined those God knew in advance would choose to accept salvation. Arminius felt that Paul was pointing this direction in Romans 8:29: "For those whom he foreknew he also predestined."

The issue for the Calvinists was the absolute sovereignty of God and the total depravity of human beings. Because we are totally depraved, they note, we cannot choose God. Because God is absolutely sovereign, God's decisions are never contingent upon what human beings do. Further, Calvinists argue that if human beings "choose" Christ of their own "free will," then this choice itself is a "work" that leads to our salvation.

Wesley, following Arminius, believed that if God predestines some people to eternal damnation based on nothing they have done and solely on God's purposes, then God is unjust, and God could never be unjust. Further, Wesley believed that the much broader witness of Scripture is that God loves the world, that Jesus came to seek and save the lost, and that God desires all to be saved. Wesley believed that God considers all who will one day choose Christ to be among the elect, and they are only able to choose Christ because of God's prevenient grace at work in their lives. That prevenient grace is available to all and at work in all, but not everyone chooses to respond to it. In 1 Timothy 2:4, the author writes that God "desires everyone to be saved and to come to the knowledge of the truth." Wesley believed that the Spirit is already at work among the lost by means of God's prevenient grace. What the lost need is someone to share the good news with them. Some will accept the good news, and others will reject it. Those who accept it are the elect by virtue of their accepting God's grace, and those who reject it reject the life Christ offers.

Wesley's passions ran deep when it came to predestination, as do the passions of many Methodist pastors today. I find it unfathomable that God would intentionally create human beings for the purpose of eternally tormenting them in hell. And these are not just a few human beings; according to Calvin's version of predestination (so-called "double predestination"), the vast majority of the human race will be eternally tormented in hell, and this apparently is God's will, since they had no chance to choose life. We often use the analogy, as Scripture does, of God loving us as parents love their children. I have two daughters, and I cannot imagine deciding before they were born that I would love one and reject the other. I cannot imagine deciding this after they were born. I love them both dearly, regardless of what they do. But let's assume, according to Calvin's views, that one of my daughters was chosen before the foundation of the world for heaven, and the other for eternal torment. How could I love a God who had assigned my daughter to eternal damnation based upon nothing she had done, giving her no opportunity to accept his grace and the salvation Christ offers?

Either or both of my daughters might reject God's grace. Though I would grieve that decision terribly, I would know they at least had been offered grace and the gift of eternal life. But the idea that God would predetermine their fate and deny them a chance to receive his love and mercy is, to me, an offense to God's honor, justice, and love. The overarching story of Scripture seems to show that God calls the Israelites to know, love, and serve him, and that human beings often turn from his path. Far from God's predetermined will, this act of turning from his path grieves God. (See Genesis 6:6 as an example.)

Repeatedly in Scripture, God calls people to repent, turn to him, choose the path of life, and do the right thing. These calls seem to indicate that we are not mere puppets, but that human beings, by the grace of God, have the ability to choose good or evil, faith or unbelief.

Wesley spent his life traveling by horseback, and in his later years by carriage, to nearly every town and village across England and at times into Ireland, Scotland, and Wales, offering Christ to sinners. During the many years when he was rejected by his colleagues and not permitted to preach in their churches, he would go to the center of town where often there stood a "market cross," and from its steps he would preach to the crowds. He preached atop gravestones, including his own father's, and on hilltops and anywhere else he could draw a crowd and be heard. He was beaten, harassed, and at times pummeled with eggs, rotten vegetables, and even rocks. He did this for decades. Why? Because he believed that God "desires everyone to be saved and to come to the knowledge of the truth."

A Passion for Finding the Lost

Predestination is a complex subject, and the brief discussion above is inadequate to flesh out the full debate between the Arminians and the Calvinists regarding election. I simply want you to catch a glimpse of this doctrinal issue, learn a bit of Wesley's thinking on it and passion around it, and consider how it affected the man and his ministry. Wesley was willing to do whatever he could to share Christ with those who did not know him. Wesley believed passionately that God longs for human beings to know the love and grace of the Creator, and that God uses people like you and me as instruments to help these lost children find their way home.

Many churches today no longer have a passion for helping lost people find their way home. Our world is becoming increasingly secular. We live in a post-Christian culture. It's likely that more than half the people in the community where you live are not actively involved in a church family. They may be nominally Christian or not Christian at all. Does God care about these people? Would their lives be different if they knew of God's love and acceptance, and they lived each day walking in grace while pursuing Christ's mission?

As I look back over my life, the best parts all have something to do with the love of God. My choice to follow God has made me a better husband to my wife, a better father to my children, and a better human being. I'm less of a jerk than I would have been otherwise. I care about things I would not have cared about. I give my resources to causes and groups that are trying to make the world a better place. My values, ideals, and ethics are all very different because of the decision I made as a fourteen-year-old boy to accept Christ. I've got a long way to go in all these areas, but I'm a different man because of that decision to accept God's grace. Truly, I have found "life in his name" (John 20:31).

We lament that many of our churches are no longer growing. Part of it is demographics, since many of our churches are located in rural areas where populations are in decline. Part of it is a lack of vitality in our music, preaching, and small groups. But I'm convinced that a big part of it is that we've lost our passion to do whatever it takes to reach those who don't yet know Christ. That passion drove Wesley and our forebears to preach on the hilltops, at the market crosses, in the cemeteries, and wherever they could get a hearing, in order to share the good news of God's grace and love for *all* people.

Len

Len was my stepfather from the time I was eleven to when I was seventeen. He was a good man who taught me a lot about life. He had a big heart. I loved the guy . . . except when he was drinking. He could be a funny drunk until he was pushed. But if he got angry, it was not good. He left my mom and our family when I was a junior in high school. Over the years I would hear from him from time to time. The alcohol destroyed his life, career, relationships, and health. But under the surface there was still that affable, good, and kind man.

Len would call me from time to time, usually a bit tipsy. He would ask about the church and my family. We'd chat for a bit, and then, before I got off the phone, I'd tell him I was praying for him. One of my regrets is not being more direct in talking with Len about Christ. He had been baptized when I was in high school; I'd even given him a Bible. Then our paths parted. He moved. I married. For years we didn't see one another. But I always felt that someday I would sit down and talk with him about God's love and invite him to choose Christ once more. That day never came.

Len died this past fall. There was no obituary in the paper, no formal service planned. His passing came, and few noticed or cared. To many, he was just a drunken, broken-down carpenter. The weekend he died, my mom, siblings, and I were together on vacation. We stopped to remember and celebrate Len's life, just the twelve of us in the living room. As I thought about Len, the Scripture that came to mind was Luke 15:1-2: "Now all the tax collectors and sinners were coming near to listen to him. And the Pharisees and the scribes were grumbling and saying, 'This fellow welcomes sinners and eats with them.'"

I found myself crying as I read the Scripture, because it represented both what I love about Jesus and the hope I had for Len: that Jesus, himself a carpenter and carpenter's son, might welcome a broken-down carpenter, a sinner who I think knew deep inside that he needed a savior. I can't say with certainty what happens with guys like Len at their death. I can say with certainty that Jesus is a friend of sinners and drunkards, and his time here on earth was focused on reaching those who were lost. And I can say that I let Len down, and let Christ down, by not making the time to sit down with Len and talk with him about his faith.

Wesley preached in city squares, on hills beside coal mines, in jails and fields. He sought out those who were nonreligious and nominally religious, and he invited them to receive God's grace and salvation through Jesus Christ, free for all. John Nelson, a stonemason who heard Wesley preach and wrote about it in his journal, gave perhaps the best description we have of Wesley's preaching:

> As soon as he got upon the stand he stroked back his hair and turned his face toward where I stood, and, I thought, fixed his eyes upon me. His countenance struck such an awful dread upon me, before I heard him speak, that it made my heart beat like the pendulum of a clock, and when he did speak I thought his whole discourse was aimed at me.[9]

Nelson came to faith under Wesley's urging. We shouldn't be surprised to learn that later, he himself became a Methodist preacher.

The Invitation: Open the Gift and Answer the Call

From April 2, 1739, until shortly before his death fifty-two years later, it is estimated that Wesley traveled—on foot, on horseback, and later by carriage—250,000 miles or more across Great Britain to preach, most often out of doors. During that time he averaged about fifteen sermons a week and over 40,000 sermons total. It was the Spirit's power and Wesley's sheer determination to offer Christ to all who would listen that drove the revival.

But Wesley didn't do it alone. It was done by all who heard him preach, who felt called to revive the faith of people in Great Britain, in America, and wherever Methodism spread. These people longed to see their lives changed by God's grace. They wanted to renew the church of their day and transform the world. The revival that took place during the eighteenth and nineteenth centuries happened because of the men and women who answered God's call to preach, teach, and minister to the multitudes.

I was sixteen when I felt called to be a pastor, but I was a freshman in college when I read about John Wesley's ministry and vision. I was drawn to Wesley's approach to the gospel, the things I've been describing in this book. I joined a United Methodist church and began moving toward ordination as a pastor. By the time I was twenty-four, I had a deep longing to start a new church that would reach nonreligious and nominally religious people, to see their lives changed, to be a part of renewing churches, and to send Christians out to transform our world.

Some of you reading this book have the gifts and call to be a pastor or full-time minister in the church. Have you considered whether God may be calling you? The key to revival in The United Methodist Church or any other denomination is gifted young people who, though they could pick any life path, decide to devote their lives to sharing God's grace, calling people to faith in Christ, and renewing churches. The Apostle Paul wrote in Romans 10:13-15:

> For, "Everyone who calls on the name of the Lord shall be saved." But how are they to call on one in whom they have not believed? And how are they to believe in one of whom they have never heard? And how are they to hear without someone to proclaim him? And how are they to proclaim him unless they are sent? As it is written, "How beautiful are the feet of those who bring good news."

You may not be called to be a pastor but may simply want to share with others what God has done in your life. God is calling all of us to this kind of ministry. Whether you are a pastor or layperson, God calls you to share your faith with family, friends, neighbors, and any with whom you have influence. Peter speaks of doing this with "gentleness and respect" (1 Peter 3:15 NIV). Our most profound witness is how we live and how we love, but at some point it also includes our words, sharing the story of what God has done in and for us.

Several years ago, a woman in our congregation made me the most amazing white chocolate cheesecake. She used the finest ingredients. She put white chocolate shavings all over the outside. It was beautifully and lovingly prepared. It must have taken her hours to bake. She brought it to the church in a beautiful box, gave it to one of our staff, and said, "This is for Pastor Adam." I was not in the office that day, so the staff member placed it in the refrigerator in the sacristy of our church. She planned to tell me about it but forgot. Six weeks later, the woman wrote me a note and said, "Did you like the cheesecake? I never heard back from you and just wanted to make sure it was okay." I had no idea what she was talking about. Later that week, we found the cheesecake in the sacristy refrigerator, with the bow still wrapped around the unopened box!

Christ offers us the gift of salvation—a word that is full of life and deep meaning. The gift came at great cost to him. The gift was for you and for everyone you know. I would ask: Have you opened the gift? Have you accepted God's grace? And, knowing that Christ has asked you to share the gift with others, have you told them about it? Don't wait until it's too late to share the story of God's amazing grace.

Who is God calling you to share his love with this week?

What to See in Bristol

Today, about a million people live in Bristol and the surrounding countryside. The city is about 100 miles west of London. If you are traveling from London, plan to visit the prehistoric monument known as Stonehenge on the trip. It's a bit out of the way but not far, and it's worth it.

In Bristol, visit the New Room, the first Methodist preaching house. The two societies that merged and became known as the United Society built the New Room, and it still stands. Completed in 1739, this was where Methodism was organized, and Wesley spent much time here. You'll find a chapel on the main floor, and above it on the second floor are meeting rooms and guest rooms, one of which was Wesley's personal residence when in Bristol. The New Room is a magnificent site. Even better is to be a part of a service held here. For information go to www.newroombristol.org.uk.

New Room preaching house

These photos show the interior of the preaching house on the main floor and Wesley's apartment on the second floor. While in Bristol, make sure also to visit Charles Wesley's home. Charles lived in Bristol from 1756 to 1771 and ultimately settled in London, where he died in 1788.

John Wesley's apartment at the New Room

Just five miles east of the New Room is Hanham Mount, Kingswood. The Kingswood mines have long since closed, and neighborhoods now surround the area where John Wesley and George Whitefield preached, but a park at the top of Hanham Mount still commemorates the site. Standing at the open-air pulpit marking the place where these Methodist preachers once stood, you can easily imagine the miners and their families coming "to the waters" to drink of the gospel that Wesley and Whitefield offered.

Hanham Mount, Kingswood

5.
Works of Mercy
The Foundry, London

What good is it, my brothers and sisters, if you say you have faith but do not have works? Can faith save you? If a brother or sister is naked and lacks daily food, and one of you says to them, "Go in peace; keep warm and eat your fill," and yet you do not supply their bodily needs, what is the good of that? So faith by itself, if it has no works, is dead. But someone will say, "You have faith and I have works." Show me your faith apart from your works, and I by my works will show you my faith.

(James 2:14-18)

By grace you have been saved through faith, and this is not your own doing; it is the gift of God—not the result of works, so that no one may boast. For we are what he has made us, created in Christ Jesus for good works, which God prepared beforehand to be our way of life.

(Ephesians 2:8-10)

5.

Works of Mercy

The Foundry, London

In this chapter we will focus our attention on what Wesley called "works of mercy," which were so integrally linked to his own faith and to the practices encouraged in the Methodist revival. We've learned that John Wesley traveled over 250,000 miles on foot, on horseback, and by carriage, often preaching out of doors in the streets and fields and markets, proclaiming the good news of God's love and grace and calling people to trust in Christ and to be born anew. His emphasis on yielding one's life to Christ, experiencing conversion, and practicing a personal faith has led many to label his faith "evangelical."

Too often, Christians have thought that the goal of faith is to be born anew and cultivate a "personal relationship with Jesus Christ." Wesley considered this goal to be an essential part of the Christian life, but he also believed that focusing solely on one's personal relationship with Jesus makes for an incomplete faith—narcissism masquerading as Christian spirituality. As Christians, our salvation is from narcissism, indifference, sin, and death, and it is *for* good works.

It's what Paul was teaching in the passage from Ephesians that Wesley preached from so many times: "For by grace you have been saved through faith, and this is not your own doing; it is the gift of God— not the result of works, so that no one may boast. For we are what he has made us, created in Christ Jesus *for good works*, which God prepared beforehand to be *our way of life*" (Ephesians 2:8-10, emphasis added).

I've italicized part of verse 10, because it's the focus of this chapter. Paul wrote that we were created "for good works," which God intended to be "our way of life." For Wesley, faith and good works were inseparable, so much so that many accused him of preaching salvation by works, which is sometimes referred to as works righteousness. But Wesley, like Paul, was clear that our works are a response to salvation and the clear fruit of that salvation.

In the previous chapter I described a young woman whose father never would affirm his love for her and never was satisfied with what she had done. She was always operating out of a deficit with her dad, trying to win his affection. Contrast that with another woman I know whose father loved her dearly, doted on her when she was little, and regularly expressed his affection for her. Her acts of love toward her father weren't meant to convince him she was worthy but instead were a heartfelt expression of gratitude for a love she had known long before she could even respond.

We've learned that Wesley believed the goal of Christian life was sanctification, being perfected in Christian love. There are two sides of sanctification: loving God with your whole heart, soul, mind, and strength; and loving your neighbor as you love yourself. Jesus said these summarized the law and the prophets. Jesus gave a second command, which he also said summarized the law and the prophets: "In everything do to others as you would have them do to you" (Matthew 7:12). We know this command as the Golden Rule.

Martin Luther once famously called the Book of James "an epistle of straw" for its emphasis on works and its seeming derision of Paul's great doctrine of justification by grace through faith. Wesley, by contrast, did not have a problem with it. He rightly understood that James was describing the heart of God and that God's salvation is not merely from sin and death but for righteousness, godliness, and works of mercy and compassion.

There are two senses in which Wesley spoke of and pursued good works. The first sense was in the ordinary expressions of love that are summarized in the Golden Rule. As we grow in sanctification, that growth should be evident in our increased patience, kindness, goodness, gentleness, and love. But if we are not consciously praying for and seeking these fruits of the spirit, they may actually diminish over time.

The second sense was in what were traditionally called "works of mercy." In Roman Catholic theology, these were divided into seven corporal works of mercy and seven spiritual works of mercy. The corporal works were largely drawn from Jesus' Parable of the Sheep and the Goats: feed the hungry, provide drink for the thirsty, clothe the naked, care for the homeless, visit the sick, and minister to the prisoner. (The seventh was burying the dead, which was drawn from Catholic scripture called the Book of Tobit). The spiritual works of mercy were instructing the ignorant, counseling those who doubted, admonishing sinners, bearing wrongs patiently, forgiving others willingly, comforting the afflicted, and praying for others. Wesley, borrowing the designation 'works of mercy,' spoke of all these and others as acts by which we intentionally care for and assist those who need God's help.

Wesley believed that with these acts of mercy, God is working in and through us. Yet he also taught that these acts of mercy are themselves a means of grace. By intentionally helping, ministering to, and caring for others, we avail ourselves of God's grace. Our own actions become the instrument God uses to change us.

You no doubt have experienced this kind of grace. Maybe you initially hesitated in volunteering to help someone, but in the midst of serving, your eyes were opened, you found joy, and your heart was filled with grace by the very actions in which you sought to share grace with others. For me, some of the most profound experiences of God's grace and love have come when I was serving others. When churches stop actively serving others—the elderly, the young, the sick, the prisoners, the hungry, the poor, those on the margins—something in those churches and in their people begins to die.

Spiritual vitality, whether in individuals or congregations, is achieved by living out the Scriptures shown at the beginning of this chapter: Ephesians 2:8-10 and James 2:14-18. Two dimensions of Christian life described in those Scriptures are critical for revival: a personal faith actively pursued through prayer, worship, Scripture reading, receiving the Eucharist, meeting in small groups, and practicing other Christian disciplines; and an invitation for God to work through you in serving your neighbor, your community, and the world. These two dimensions, taken together, constitute the holistic gospel that Jesus taught and preached, and they constitute the holistic gospel that Wesley insisted was "the scripture way of salvation."

Eight years before Wesley's heart-warming experience of God's grace on Aldersgate Street, he had already begun practicing acts of mercy as an essential part of his faith. It was actually one of the Oxford students with whom he had met to study Scripture, William Morgan, who encouraged Wesley to do so. Morgan had been visiting prisoners at the Castle Prison in Oxford and asked Wesley to join him. Soon John, too, was ministering to prisoners. Richard Heitzenrater points out Wesley's scheme for pastoral visitation for 1731, taken from Wesley's diary: "Monday, Bocardo [Prison]; Tuesday, Castle [Prison]; Wednesday, children; Thursday, Castle; Friday, Bocardo; Saturday, Castle; Sunday, poor and elderly."[1] These simple entries and humble actions became defining elements of

Methodism: ministering to prisoners, helping impoverished children, visiting the elderly, caring for the poor.

After Wesley joined Whitefield in preaching to the Kingswood miners, both men felt called to begin a school for the poor children of miners and for anyone else, regardless of age, who wished to learn. Wesley built a schoolhouse that was used both for education and as a preaching house. This was not the first time Wesley and the Methodists had been involved in educating underprivileged children; as with prison ministry, he and the others at Oxford had begun an education ministry, pooling their resources to hire a tutor for children there.

Education was important to the early Methodists. It was a ticket out of poverty and also a tool that made students more effective instruments for God's use in changing the world. As Methodism spread in eighteenth- and nineteenth-century America, the tradition continued. In my hometown of Kansas City, Missouri, one of the first public schools began in the basement of the Westport Methodist Church. About that same time, Methodists started one of the first public schools in Kansas, just across the state line only a few miles from Westport. That school, the Shawnee Methodist Mission, was for Native American children.

In addition to public schools, American Methodists started hundreds of colleges and universities. It's likely that in your state, perhaps in your own town, there's an institution of higher learning that was founded by Methodists. Universities started by Methodists include Southern Methodist (listed first because it's my alma mater!), Duke, Emory, Northwestern, Drew, Boston University, and the University of Southern California, to name just a few of the better known schools. The impulse to start universities should not surprise us, given that the Methodist movement began with an Oxford fellow and a small group of college students.

Freeing Prisoners

Knowing that prison ministry goes back to the beginning of Methodism, I wonder if your church is involved in visiting prisoners. This has been a rich and rewarding part of our ministry at the Church of the Resurrection. One of the people participating in this ministry is Ron Smith. Here is how he describes his experience:

> After retiring from law enforcement I had many reservations about getting involved in prison ministry. But these guys are just like us, broken and in need of help, and certainly in need of spiritual healing. Many of them just wanted to have a relationship with someone who cared, someone who saw them as human, and someone who was willing to help. That touched me deeply. Of all the things that I've done in my life, being involved in prison ministry—helping young men and women get their lives back on track—makes everything else pale in comparison. It's salvaging families. It's salvaging lives. It's resurrecting communities. It's giving people hope. What else would Christians do?

Ron is being used by God, along with all the other men and women in our prison ministry. They are "salvaging lives." And in the process, Ron and the others are being perfected in love.

The Foundry in London: Two Sides of the Gospel

Upon returning from America, having been challenged and encouraged by the faith of the Moravian Christians, Wesley spent much of his time in London during 1738, helping to form a religious society that became known as the Fetter Lane Society. As we've learned, religious societies were organizations of like-minded Christians who sought to encourage one another toward spiritual health and maturity. They met once a week for prayer and mutual accountability. Wesley described this group as the "third rise of Methodism" (the first being at Oxford, the second being with the fledgling groups he led in Georgia).[2]

By the fall of 1739, there were growing divisions in the Fetter Lane Society over various points of faith and practice. In November, Wesley had preached outdoors to seven or eight thousand people at the former site of a cannon foundry that was dilapidated and in disrepair. The building was purchased and renovated and would become the home of Methodism in London for the next thirty-eight years. A new society was founded at the renovated building, now known as the Foundry. This society eventually took on the same name as the combined groups in Bristol: the United Society. This was the name by which the Methodist societies became known throughout Great Britain.

At the Foundry in the 1740s, the Methodist works of mercy saw new expressions. Wesley started a fund to make small loans, akin to today's microlending, and the fund made loans to 250 people in the first year. On Fridays, the poor who were sick came to be treated and were provided basic medical care. In 1747, Wesley published a book on "easy and natural" methods for "curing most diseases." Wesley and the Methodists at the Foundry leased two houses for poor and elderly widows and their children. And, as at Kingswood, they started a school for children who roamed the streets.

Hundreds if not thousands of inner-city ministries, medical clinics, hospitals, orphanages, and more have been started across the United States, Great Britain, and around the world by Methodists who are carrying on traditions established at the Foundry. Christians in the Wesleyan tradition continue to go on mission trips and serve in medical clinics around the world. They advocate access to health care for low-income people. They seek to

> Speak out for those who cannot speak,
>> for the rights of all the destitute.
> Speak out, judge righteously,
>> defend the rights of the poor and needy. (Proverbs 31:8-9)

For Wesley, evangelism and ministries to the poor were inextricably linked; you could not have one without the other. It was this linkage that I found so exciting when I first visited a United Methodist church during my freshman year in college. I was eighteen years old and had been a part of a wonderful church that sought to help me grow in my love for God. I had been taught to read and memorize Scripture. I had attended worship on Sunday morning, Sunday night, and Wednesday night. I had taken part in outreach and mission, which for us was to tell others about Jesus. I had learned to care for others in the church. But I had heard little about serving those in need outside our church or embodying the presence of Christ in the community to meet the needs of others.

In the United Methodist church I visited, by contrast, members were busily engaged in serving the poor, repairing houses for the elderly, and visiting prisons. They hosted food pantries, medical missions, and support groups for people who had never been to the church but nonetheless needed support. I found their efforts inspiring and compelling.

Jesus spoke a lot about the kingdom of God. In one sense that kingdom is all of creation, and God is the "King of the Universe," a phrase my Jewish friends use to address God. But human existence has been marked by rebellions against God. From Adam and Eve on, people have regularly turned aside from God's will (a practice we call sin), with the result that human history is littered with wars, acts of inhumanity, and injustice. As we say in the prayer of confession that often accompanies the Eucharist, "We have not loved you with our whole heart. We have not loved our neighbors as ourselves." So when Jesus speaks about the kingdom of God, he is usually articulating a vision not of what life is but of what it should be. Through new birth and the sanctifying work of the Spirit, we seek to reflect that kingdom in our lives.

We pray, "Thy kingdom come, thy will be done, on earth as it is in heaven," and we're meant to work and act accordingly. As we look around us, we see the gap between the world as it is and the world as it should be. That's when we ask, "Lord, what would you have us do to close that gap?" In the world as it should be, no one goes to bed hungry because they don't have enough to eat. No one is cold because they don't have clothing and shelter. In the world as it should be, all are treated with respect and compassion and receive justice. There are no wars, no one receives a subpar education, and racism and bigotry have vanished. If that is the world as it should be, then Christians are meant to work to close the gap between the realities of the world we live in and Christ's vision of God's kingdom on earth. This means that our task as Christians is to feed the hungry, clothe the naked, welcome strangers, provide quality education for low-income children, minister to the sick who can't afford medical care, and so much more.

What's interesting is that in today's world, young adults who have turned away from "organized religion" are joining groups engaged in helping the world look like the Kingdom of God. They may not use those words, but it's a driving passion of many young adults who don't go to church. And when the church is actually *being* the church, engaged in serving others and not simply focused on individual salvation, then young adults begin to see the church in a different light. At our church, we've found that many young adults first come because we are engaged in community ministry, and then, as they participate in that ministry, they encounter the good news of Jesus Christ. These are two sides of the same gospel.

Unfortunately, in the twentieth century there was a tendency to separate the two sides of the gospel. "Liberal" churches focused on doing amazing work to serve others but often forgot evangelism. Wesley believed that the poor needed not just food and clothing but assurance that God loved them and that God's grace could pardon their sins and make them new.

In contrast, "conservative" churches preached and taught personal salvation and invited their members to accept Christ and grow in their love for God, but often left aside the social gospel and the call not just to pray for God's kingdom but to work actively toward achieving it. They cared for the poor among their membership but were less engaged in ministries of compassion, mercy, and justice in the surrounding community.

This wasn't the only split between two sides of the gospel. Some churches focused on the intellectual faith that was so important to Wesley, but they overlooked his emphasis on experiential faith, a faith of the warmed heart, as though passion and fervor were a bit embarrassing to them. Conversely, other churches retained the spiritual fervor and enthusiasm of the early Methodist movement but downplayed intellectual dimensions of the faith, as if afraid that intellect would sap them of spiritual vitality. One sign of this split was that some Wesleyan traditions that valued the intellect required their clergy to have a master's degree from an approved seminary, while those that valued the heart were often willing to ordain people with no formal education, even believing that seminary might douse the spiritual fire of their clergy. As with the liberal-conservative divide, the head-heart dichotomy left each side with only half the gospel.

I believe that individuals, churches, and denominations who hold together the social and evangelical gospels, and who embrace a religion of both the intellect and the heart, come nearest to Wesley's emphasis and to the religion that follows Christ's two great commandments.

Wesley's approach to the Christian faith is sometimes described as dialectical—holding in tension two things that appear to be opposites and forging a synthesis of the two that makes for a stronger and more complete faith than either side had alone. Once again, this is what we see in Jesus' great commandments to love God and love neighbor.

Because of Wesley's dialectical approach, Methodism is sometimes referred to as a church of both/and rather than either/or. When people ask me if I'm liberal or conservative, my answer is always the same: Yes! Being conservative means valuing tradition, holding fast to timeless truths even when they are no longer in fashion. Being liberal means showing a generous spirit, being open to reform and willing to see things in new ways. At our best, we hold both of these impulses together. The evangelical gospel without the social gospel becomes spiritual narcissism; the social gospel without the evangelical gospel fails to address the root problem of the human condition and leaves us without the power to be transformed and renewed by Christ.

The Christian life begins as our hearts are drawn to God through God's prevenient grace. It progresses as we hear the good news and choose to trust in Jesus Christ and receive his justifying grace and a new birth. However, this birth is not the end of our faith; it is when the real journey begins. As we experience the means of grace, we're restored by the Spirit to become what God has made us to be: created in God's image, loving God with all that is within us, and blessing our neighbor with a love not merely of words or affections but also of deeds expressing compassion, mercy, and justice.

Wesley knew that loving God and neighbor are two integrally connected sides of the gospel. They are what Paul was speaking of in one of the Scriptures that began this chapter:

> By grace you have been saved through faith, and this is not your own doing; it is the gift of God—not the result of works, so that no one may boast. For we are what he has made us, *created in Christ Jesus for good works, which God prepared beforehand to be our way of life.* (Ephesians 2:8-10, emphasis added)

Do you have a "both/and" faith? Do you recognize the importance of both a personal walk with Christ and a gospel that is lived out by good works? Do you seek to love God with your mind, your heart, and your strength? Does your faith reflect both sides of the gospel?

Sites Associated with Wesley's Works of Mercy

When you visit Oxford you can see the Castle Prison, where Wesley visited prisoners on hundreds of occasions during his time in Oxford. If money is not an object, you can stay at the Malmaison Hotel, which purchased a part of the Castle Prison and created an upscale hotel where the prisoners once slept. If you aren't able to spend the night there, at least plan to have a meal in the Malmaison (www.malmaison.com/locations/oxford/).

Castle Prison

Many of the sites mentioned in this chapter no longer exist as they were in Wesley's day. The Kingswood School in Bristol has relocated, though you can still see a bell at the present location that was cast from the original Kingswood School bell. In London, not far from City Road Chapel (today known as Wesley's Chapel), you can find a plaque marking the site of the Foundry.

Bell cast from original Kingswood School bell

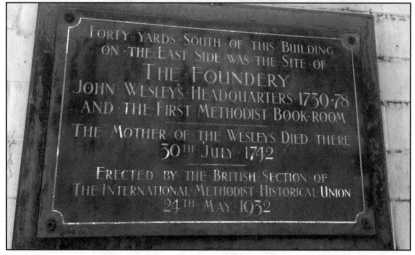

Plaque marking the site of the Foundry

6.

Persevering to the End
City Road Chapel, London

"Blessed are those who are persecuted for righteousness' sake, for theirs is the kingdom of heaven. Blessed are you when people revile you and persecute you and utter all kinds of evil against you falsely on my account. Rejoice and be glad, for your reward is great in heaven, for in the same way they persecuted the prophets who were before you."

(Matthew 5:10-12)

Speak out for those who cannot speak,
*   for the rights of all the destitute.*
Speak out, judge righteously,
*   defend the rights of the poor and needy.*

(Proverbs 31:8-9)

6.

Persevering to the End

City Road Chapel, London

Jesus promised his disciples there would be opposition to their ministry: "In the world you face persecution. But take courage; I have conquered the world!" (John 16:33). When you have a vision, some will oppose it. When you challenge the status quo, you'll ruffle feathers. When you are passionate, others will be skeptical. When you see a measure of success, some will find you threatening. When you seek to change things, you'll encounter resistance.

As John and Charles Wesley preached in the fields, challenging the spiritual malaise of the Anglican Church in the eighteenth century and passionately calling their hearers to a deeper faith and a holier life, they roused opposition. In this chapter we will consider that opposition, which marked the middle period of John Wesley's life, and Wesley's response to it. We will then contemplate Wesley's final years, when his opponents quieted and Methodism entered a more mature period. During that final phase, among his concerns were opposition to slavery, the Christian use of money, ways to face death with faith, and how to leave a lasting legacy.

Opposition, Persecution, and Perseverance

As we've seen, the Wesleys' preaching was unnerving to many of the priests and laity who heard them. These listeners were unsettled by the Wesleys' zeal and passion and were challenged by their sometimes condemning and convicting words. Consider how John Wesley concluded his sermon "Scriptural Christianity," which he preached in 1744 at St. Mary's Church in Oxford. It was the last time he would be invited to preach there.

> May it not be one of the consequences of this that so many of you are a generation of *triflers*; triflers with God, with one another, and with your own souls? For how few of you spend, from one week to another, a single hour in private prayer? How few have any thought of God in the general tenor of your conversation? Who of you is in any degree acquainted with the work of his Spirit? His supernatural work in the souls of men? Can you bear, unless now and then in a church, any talk of the Holy Ghost? Would you not take it for granted if one began such a conversation that it was either "hypocrisy" or "enthusiasm"? In the name of the Lord God Almighty I ask, What religion are *you* of? Even the talk of Christianity ye cannot, will not, bear. O my brethren! What a Christian city is this? "It is time for thee, Lord, to lay to thine hand!"[1]

These were harsh and presumptive words, spoken to a chapel filled with ordained clergy and many students who were pursuing orders.

Wesley challenged listeners throughout England (and Scotland, Ireland, and Wales) to a deeper level of commitment and a serious pursuit of a holy life. Wesley said that many who thought they were

Christians seemed to be so in name only; they were almost Christians. They did not have the joy, assurance, or peace that comes from being wholly surrendered to God. They lived their lives in compromise with sin, willing to do just enough good but no more. They entertained evil, provided that it wasn't too extreme. They did little or nothing to grow in love with God.

In what ways did faith in the church of Wesley's day resemble the faith in our churches today? Some would suggest in a great many ways.

Wesley said there is so much more to being a Christian than simple acceptance; there is a power, love, and joy that come from walking with God. And God expects more of Christians than simply trying to not be so bad as other people.

Because of Wesley's challenging style and message, many churches were closed to him, so he began preaching in the fields and marketplaces, often quite near the churches that had shut their doors to him. As we've learned, most towns with a market had a market cross at the center as a visible reminder to merchants that Christ watched as they conducted business. Wesley often preached on the stairs or near these crosses. He would start by singing hymns until a crowd had gathered, then he would begin to preach about the need for salvation, forgiveness, and waking to God.

The priests and laity offended by his sermons often were the same people who hired thugs and rabble-rousers to disturb him. Many of the priests felt Wesley was preaching without authorization and meddling with the people in their town. Wesley kept a daily journal, and you can read about hundreds of such clashes. Here's one example from August 28, 1748, when Wesley preached at the market cross in Bolton, England:

At one I went to the cross in Bolton. There was a vast number of people, but many of them utterly wild. As soon as I began speaking, they began thrusting to and fro, endeavoring to throw me down from the steps on which I stood. They did so once or twice, but I went up again and continued my discourse. They then began to throw stones; at the same time some got upon the cross behind me to push me down.[2]

Wesley described how he got right back up and continued preaching, silencing the crowd. You may remember that John's father, Samuel, taught him perseverance. During nineteen years of sermons, John was pelted with rotten tomatoes, manure, and stones, but he refused to give up.

In every crowd, though, were those who heard Wesley and were moved. He described the work of the Holy Spirit among the mobs and his often miraculous deliverance from harm. He reported that frequently those who came like lions to devour him left like lambs, and many found their own souls awakened by the Spirit through his preaching.

For nineteen years this was Wesley's weekly, even daily experience. He was dragged before magistrates, beaten with fists, pummeled with rocks. Homes where he stayed were set afire. How discouraging it must have been. But he refused to give up, and his perseverance in the face of opposition made all the difference.

I was speaking with a young pastor recently who was leaving his church after just one year. He had gone there hoping to build a future for the dying church. But the longtime members of the church criticized every change he proposed and every new idea he offered. This gifted pastor was so discouraged that he had given up hope of being able to serve the congregation and had even begun questioning his own calling as a pastor. The experience is shared by many pastors I meet and by many laypeople in their workplaces.

A couple of years ago I was invited to deliver the message at the Inaugural Prayer Service for President Obama's second term. This is a special worship service held on the morning of the president's first full day in office after the inauguration—a tradition dating back to George Washington. As I prayed and contemplated what the Lord's word might be for the president, vice president, and members of the administration, I thought of how leaders over the years have grown discouraged because of opposition and criticism. I reminded the president that every leader faces this same difficulty. I pointed to Moses, who at one time was so discouraged by the Israelites' complaining and grumbling that he prayed, in essence, "God, kill me now! I don't want to keep leading these people" (see Numbers 11:10-15). Imagine if Moses had given up that day and returned to tending goats.

I went on to recount an experience of Martin Luther King Jr. that took place in January 1956.[3] Late one night he received a threatening phone call. It was not the first he had received, but that particular night, feeling exhausted physically and emotionally, he became so discouraged that he considered bowing out of leadership in the civil rights movement. Sitting at the kitchen table, he prayed to God, saying he was afraid and was at the end of his strength. At that moment, he experienced God's presence as he never had before. He heard God's voice telling him to keep standing up for truth and righteousness. That experience strengthened him for his work. Imagine if Dr. King had bowed out of leadership that night, rather than pressing on with the fight for civil rights. Where would our nation be?

Here's the Question

If you're in the workplace and try to lead your organization to change, there will be people who oppose you, perhaps even hate you. If you stand up for what you believe when everyone else is against you—even if you try to do so with tact and gentleness—people may say bad things about you.

I recall a particularly difficult time in my own ministry, more than ten years ago, when I felt like giving up. I'd preached a sermon that led several hundred people to leave our church. I'd received notes and e-mails expressing disappointment in me. I remember telling my wife one evening, "LaVon, I don't want to do this anymore. It's too hard." She wisely asked, "Is God calling you to quit, or are you simply giving up?" She told me she would be by my side whatever I did, but her words stuck with me. I had not felt God calling me to quit; I was just discouraged and wanted to give up. So I continued to press forward, asking God to give me strength and to lead me as I sought to lead the church. It was several months before the feelings of discouragement lifted. In the years since, I've experienced so many blessings and exciting moments of ministry through our church, all of which I would have missed had I quit when things were difficult.

There will be times in your life when people oppose you for doing the right thing and you feel like quitting. At those times, here's the question: Is God calling you to quit, or are you simply giving up? If God is not calling you to quit, will you give up or keep going? Will you, like Wesley, brush off the manure and go at it again? The people who change the world are those who refuse to give in, who get back up when they're pushed down, who have the courage, with God's help, to keep moving forward.

John Wesley was harassed, harangued, and lampooned by thousands. Surely he felt like quitting, but he refused. What if he had stopped in 1738 when church after church closed their doors to him, or if he had given up after the Oxford sermon in 1744 on Scriptural Christianity, when the faculty and students of his alma mater harshly criticized him? Wesley's perseverance made possible the great revival led by Methodists around the world.

By 1757, nearly twenty years after returning from America, Wesley had preached thousands of sermons and the mobs had largely ceased. In rare instances he would be harassed while speaking, but generally others in the crowd would silence the hecklers. Literally millions had found their souls awakened by Wesley's field preaching. By his sixties, Wesley had become something of a celebrity and was invited to preach in nearly every pulpit throughout England! By his seventies and eighties he was a national hero, having been used by God to touch countless lives.

The great revival of Christianity took place under Wesley's leadership because he refused to give up, despite years of sometimes violent opposition. He remembered the words of Jesus in Matthew 5:11-12: "Blessed are you when people revile you and persecute you and utter all kinds of evil against you falsely on my account. Rejoice and be glad."

Charles Wesley and the Music of the Wesleyan Revival

As I noted in the introduction, the focus of this book, owing to its intended length, is John Wesley's life and faith. But the eighteenth-century Methodist revival was not led by John alone. There were many key leaders in Great Britain, America, and other places around the world. Of these leaders, no one played a greater role alongside John than his brother Charles. Charles was four years younger than John and often followed in his brother's footsteps (to Christ Church in Oxford, into the priesthood, to America, and ultimately to leadership in the Methodist movement). But it could be argued that in some ways Charles served as an important catalyst for John's ministry and actually led the way for his older brother.

While a student at Oxford, Charles asked John to mentor him and his friends in what John would later call the "first rise of Methodism." Charles experienced his own "conversion" or heart-warming experience three days before John did. John and Charles embraced field preaching, shared in the itinerant ministry, organized people into groups and societies, and had very similar theological convictions. Where Charles stood apart and made a unique contribution was in recognizing the power of music for the Spirit's work in the revival.

Duke Divinity School has an online collection of 4,400 hymns and poems that scholars identify as coming from the pen of Charles Wesley. There may be many more, but scholars seem confident in ascribing these to Charles. The hymns were Charles's poetry set to music, and the tunes were easy to sing. Words and music combined in hymns that taught and reinforced the key theological and spiritual convictions of the movement.

The hymns were moving expressions of praise and thanksgiving to God. Some of them celebrated and commemorated key moments in a Chrisitan's life. For instance, "O For a Thousand Tongues to Sing" was written to mark the first anniversary of Charles's conversion experience, yet its celebratory tone and passionate praise spoke to nearly every believer. At the other extreme, some of Charles's hymns were composed for prisoners sentenced to die, to help them as they approached the gallows. At times Charles would actually sing the hymns to the prisoners in their final moments.

In the debate concerning contemporary music in our churches, sometimes we forget that all of Charles Wesley's hymns were "contemporary" when they were written. At that time in the Anglican Church, psalms and chants were offered in the context of worship. Charles Wesley, along with a handful of others, played a key role in introducing hymns that put into everyday words and phrases the themes of the faith and the experiences believers had of God's grace.

It is still true for those who seek their own spiritual revival that singing "psalms and hymns and spiritual songs" (Ephesians 5:19) opens our hearts to the Spirit and leads us to experience a closeness to God and a spiritual passion. Often in my times of prayer I'll sing to God. I do it while taking walks or driving in my car, and certainly during corporate worship in the church. I often return to the Wesley hymns in addition to more contemporary songs of faith. In addition to "O For a Thousand Tongues to Sing," Charles Wesley's best-known hymns include "Love Divine, All Loves Excelling," "Christ the Lord Is Risen Today," "Come, Thou Long-Expected Jesus," and "Hark! the Herald Angels Sing."

John Wesley sought to give clear directions on how to sing the hymns he and Charles compiled into hymn books. Here are some of his directions, still printed in the front of *The United Methodist Hymnal*:

1. Learn these tunes before you learn any others; afterwards learn as many as you please.
2. Sing them exactly as they are printed here . . . .
3. Sing all. . . .
4. Sing lustily and with a good courage. . . .
5. Sing modestly. . . .
6. Sing in time. . . .
7. Above all sing spiritually. . . .

I find that I have to prepare for worship and singing. Often, if I take no time to prepare my heart for worship, I'll sing several songs without fully engaging my mind or heart. It is easy to sing a hymn and never once think about what we are singing, why we are singing it, or to whom we are singing. Our songs become acts of worship only when we engage our minds and hearts. If we don't, we become like those whom Jesus, and before him Isaiah, warned about: "'This people honors me with their lips, but their hearts are far from me'" (Matthew 15:8).

Nineteenth-century Methodists in America had their own hymnals, very small so as to fit into a pocket. These were considered important companions to the Bible at that time. Reading Scripture, hearing it proclaimed, and singing its precepts were all essential to the Wesleyan revival, as we can tell from Charles Wesley's most famous hymn:

O for a thousand tongues to sing my great Redeemer's praise,
the glories of my God and King, the triumphs of his grace!

I wonder, have you discovered the joy of singing your prayers and acts of worship to God?

Speaking Out for Those Who Can't Speak for Themselves

As John Wesley grew older, it would have been easy to play it safe. An elder statesman in the Christian revival, he enjoyed the favor of millions. Why rock the boat now? Yet he seemed to understand that precisely because of his stature and influence, he must, in the words of the Proverbs 31:8-9, "Speak out for those who cannot speak, for the rights of all the destitute. Speak out, judge righteously, defend the rights of the poor and needy."

Beginning in his late sixties, Wesley began to speak out against the slave trade. Many of the slave traders were British. The ships often set sail from Bristol, one of the hubs of Methodism, then traded for slaves in Africa and took them to America where the slaves were traded for tobacco, sugar, cotton, and other goods to be sold in Great Britain.

In 1774, Wesley published a widely distributed tract called "Thoughts Upon Slavery," in which he expressed strong opposition to the practice of slavery and the slave trade. In 1788, at the age of eighty-five, he preached a sermon against slavery in the New Room at Bristol. Many members of the Methodist society made their living off the slave trade in one way or another, so his sermon wasn't welcomed by all. He described in his journal what happened: "The people rushed upon each other with the utmost violence, the benches were broke in pieces, and nine-tenths of the congregation appeared to be struck with the same panic."[4] Wesley's sermon actually provoked a fight in the congregation between those for and against slavery. They didn't just exchange angry words; they were breaking up the pews! Wesley, even as an elderly man, was not afraid of offending others in proclaiming the gospel. The last letter Wesley wrote, just a short time before he died, was to William Wilberforce, encouraging him to continue the fight against slavery.

Some of you reading this book are in your sixties, seventies, and eighties. Are you speaking out for those who can't speak? Are you standing against injustice, for the rights of the poor and needy, for the dignity of those who have been pushed down or made to feel small? Or are you playing it safe and coasting in the second half of your life?

Methodism's Mother Church: City Road Chapel

As Methodism became more established, it was clear that Methodists would need places to gather for prayer, study, and worship. Hundreds of Methodist chapels and preaching houses were built during these years. Field preaching continued, but the chapels became the hub of Methodist activity.

In 1776, it was decided that the Foundry—the old cannon works in London where Methodists had met for twenty-seven years—was no longer serving the group's needs and likely would need to be torn down. Wesley started a "capital campaign" to raise money for a new chapel that would be the center of Methodism in London. He would build the chapel directly across the street from the cemetery where his mother, Susanna, had been buried.

City Road Chapel, now known as Wesley's Chapel, was finished in 1778. It is considered by many to be Methodism's "mother church" or the "cathedral of Methodism." Wesley preached there many times. He constructed a home next to the chapel and lived there, when he was not traveling, during the final twelve years of his life.

Wesley believed in caring for the poor and supporting missions, but he also believed that buildings were important as tools for drawing people to Christ and preparing the saints for ministry. When he planned a building, he hoped it would serve the needs of the people until the time Christ would return. For 235 years, City Road Chapel has been a place where lives are changed, disciples are formed, and people are equipped to go out into the world and live their faith. The church is not a building, and buildings can never be the purpose of our ministry, but buildings are important tools and, built well, can serve the church for generations to come.

Wesley's Concern About Wealth

As Wesley grew older and the Methodist movement grew larger, he became concerned about the prosperity of Methodists. Many of the early Methodists had been from the lower ranks in society, but as their lives changed, their jobs and social status also changed. Frequently the honesty, integrity, and trustworthiness that grew from their Methodism resulted in promotions, and increasingly Methodists found themselves in the middle or upper class.

Wesley feared that prosperity might lead some to fall away. In his latter years he repeatedly warned against this. One of the texts he frequently preached from was Paul's statement in 1 Timothy 6:9: "Those who want to be rich fall into temptation and are trapped by many senseless and harmful desires that plunge people into ruin and destruction."

In Wesley's sermon "The Use of Money," he offered three rules for Christians: Gain all you can. Save all you can. Give all you can.[5]

Gaining all you can means to earn all you're capable of, provided you aren't hurting yourself or others. Wesley specifically stated, "We ought not to gain money at the expense of life, nor at the expense of our health" (which is in effect the same thing). He also noted, "Our employ cannot be harmful to our neighbor, lest we violate the command to love our neighbor."

Saving all you can means to set money aside before spending frivolously or on nonessentials, and specifically not to spend just to win the admiration of others. Of indulging our desires Wesley noted, "Daily experience shows, the more they are indulged, they increase the more." He also warned those who had accumulated a vast estate not to give all of it to one's children, particularly if the children would use it only to gratify themselves. Instead, he suggested giving enough to the children to keep them from poverty, then giving the rest in whatever way would glorify God.

Finally, giving all you can means to provide for the essential needs of your family, then for the care of those in need within the church, and finally for those outside the church. For Wesley, giving the first tenth of his income to God was something of a floor for his giving, not a ceiling. Even when his income was very small he sought to live in moderation and to give away the rest.

Early in his ministry, Wesley earned thirty pounds a year. He gave away two pounds and lived on twenty-eight. The following year his salary doubled to sixty pounds. He decided to continue living on twenty-eight pounds, and he gave away thirty-two. Over the course of his life, especially because of book sales, he earned a significant income; but each year he gave away an increasing percentage of his income, amounting to about ninety percent by the time of his death.

In doing so, Wesley was teaching and modeling that holiness and a desire to serve God can be judged in part by looking at your finances. If Wesley were here today, I think he would ask, "What does your bank statement say about your spiritual life?" He might also point out that giving money, while important, is not the primary aim of the Christian life; it is merely a reflection of our faith. The aim of the Christian life is being wholly devoted to God, and loving God and neighbor, which in turn leads to financial generosity. To Wesley, tithing might be a good initial goal, but giving all you can—money, time, and heart—was the real measure.

I've found in my own spiritual life that giving is not just a reflection of my faith; it is also a means to greater faith and deeper love for God. Our giving is an expression of worship, but also a means to deeper worship. It is a sign of our faith, but it also leads to a deeper faith.

It is true that where your heart is, your treasure should follow. But Jesus said, "Where your treasure is, there your heart will be also" (Matthew 6:21). In other words, what we do with our money is not just a reflection or expression of our heart; it also helps to shape and direct our heart.

Generosity is not just a fruit of revival; it is also a means to revival. Are you a generous giver?

Wesley's Last Days and Holy Dying

Wesley lived to be eighty-seven, a very advanced age in the 1700s. Through his eighties he continued to preach outdoors; in fact, he was eighty-seven the last time he preached under a tree, in the town of Winchelsea. He spent more and more time in London the last few years of his life, living in the house the Methodists had built for him next to City Road Chapel. It was Wesley's home, but it was also home to any visiting preachers who came to London. And it was there, in his bedroom, that John Wesley breathed his last.

Wesley frequently had taught about holy dying and what constituted a good death. He had seen many saints die and told of how those who trusted in Christ faced death with hope. He encouraged people to think about their own death, and how, even in dying, they might bear witness to their faith.

Recently I was at the hospital with one of the saints of our church. He realized he was dying, and so with faith and grace he told his loved ones good-bye. He was ready. He had taught them his entire life about having hope in Christ. He told them he would see them again. He believed his last days on this earth to be one of the most powerful opportunities to bear witness to his faith. To the end, he was seeking to serve Christ and encourage others. That knowledge didn't remove the pain of parting, but it did reaffirm the hope of the gospel. His death was a testament to his faith.

A devoted believer named Elizabeth Ritchie was John Wesley's friend and housekeeper. She was with Wesley when he died and recorded the account of his passing. He had preached in City Road Chapel just a few days before. Ritchie noted that now, with Wesley unable to rise from his bed, the room was filled with the very presence of God. Surrounded by his friends, Wesley gathered his strength and said, "The best of all is, God is with us!" He repeated these words a short while later, then gathered the strength to pray aloud, "We thank thee, O Lord, for these and all thy mercies; bless the Church and King; grant us truth and peace through Jesus Christ our Lord forever and ever!"

Ritchie noted that just before Wesley died, he tried to sing an Isaac Watts hymn, "I'll Praise My Maker While I've Breath." All he could muster was "I'll praise . . . I'll praise." And then he uttered one final word to his friends: "Farewell." At eighty-seven John Wesley breathed his last.[6]

The first stanza of the hymn Wesley was trying to sing goes like this:

I'll praise my Maker while I've breath;
and when my voice is lost in death,
praise shall employ my nobler powers.
My days of praise shall ne'er be past,
while life, and thought, and being last,
or immortality endures.[7]

His was a good death. To the end, he sought to live wholly surrendered to Christ. Like Paul, he might have said, "The time of my departure has come. I have fought the good fight, I have finished the race, I have kept the faith" (2 Timothy 4:6-7). More than ten thousand people filed past Wesley's casket in City Road Chapel. Then he was carried to the graveyard behind the church, where he was laid to rest.

The End or the Beginning?

So we come to the end of Wesley's story. In many ways, though, it was not the end but only the end of the beginning. He believed that the exciting part of his journey was just starting as he entered God's eternal kingdom. And Wesley's message and approach to the Christian faith were just beginning to spread across America and other parts of the world. Over the next two hundred years, Wesley's descendants in the faith would start 40,000 Methodist churches in America alone. The fact that you are reading this book today, more than two centuries years after his death, is testimony to the continuing impact of his life.

The faith that Wesley lived engaged head, heart, and hands. It held together both the evangelical gospel, calling us to trust in Christ as Savior and Lord, and the social gospel, calling us to be God's instruments for healing in a broken world. It was characterized by a "reasonable enthusiasm"—guided by strong minds engaged in theological reflection and study, and at the same time marked by strangely warmed hearts and a deep spiritual passion. It combined a belief in the wideness of God's mercy with a call to holiness of heart and life. I believe that Wesley's faith—grace-filled, authentic, passionate, personal, practical, intellectual; shared in small groups, celebrated in worship, lived out in the world—is a faith with the power to captivate the hearts of a whole new generation of people and to bring revival in our time.

Writing this book renewed my passion for Christ and for bringing him glory in everything I do. It revived my desire for holiness. It reminded me of the need to speak out and persevere. It left me longing to see God's image reflected in me. It left me wanting God not only to restore me but to use me as an instrument. My hope and prayer is that it might have the same effect on you. After all, John Wesley asked us not to settle for being almost Christians, but rather to become altogether Christians.

There is a prayer that Wesley invited his preachers to say at the New Year. It is a prayer of complete surrender to God. I pray it, or some variation of it, every morning on my knees when I awaken. I invite you now to pray it aloud as you surrender your life to Jesus Christ.

> I am no longer my own, but thine.
> Put me to what thou wilt, rank me with whom thou wilt.
> Put me to doing, put me to suffering.
> Let me be employed for thee or laid aside for thee,
> exalted for thee or brought low for thee.
> Let me be full, let me be empty.
> Let me have all things, let me have nothing.
> I freely and heartily yield all things
> to thy pleasure and disposal.
> And now, O glorious and blessed God,
> Father, Son, and Holy Spirit,
> thou art mine, and I am thine. So be it.
> And the covenant which I have made on earth,
> let it be ratified in heaven. Amen.[8]

What to See in London

Today, over 200 years after it was built, City Road Chapel (now called Wesley's Chapel) still houses an active congregation and is a hub of Methodist activity. Next door is John Wesley's house, and Wesley's grave is behind the church. If you're in London, you'll want to visit these places. Hours and other information can be found at www.wesleyschapel.org.uk.

City Road Chapel

Interior, City Road Chapel

From the pulpit

Included inside the chapel is a balcony aimed at bringing people as close to the pulpit as possible. In a pinch it seats a thousand, but it doesn't look that big. The pulpit was Wesley's, where he preached often in the last years of his life, and it was a great privilege to step up into it. On the wall behind the pulpit are the two great commandments on either side and the Apostles' Creed in the center, and above them is a triptych of stained glass windows.

Allow several hours to see the exhibits in the basement museum under the chapel, including Charles Wesley's organ and, in the small Foundry Chapel, pews from the original Foundry.

Pews from the original Foundry

Wesley's house next door to City Road Chapel

Wesley's prayer closet

The house where Wesley spent the final years of his life is located next door to City Road Chapel and across the street from Bunhill Cemetery, where Susanna Wesley is buried. The most moving place in Wesley's house is his bedroom, with the prayer closet you see in the photo. The kneeler is said to be a reminder of where the power of the Methodist revival came from: it was the power of God that came from the prayers of Wesley and so many others. From this room Wesley could look out at the chapel as he prayed for God's continuing work among the Methodists. And it was in this room that Wesley breathed his last.

Susanna Wesley's grave in Bunhill Cemetery

John Wesley's grave

Don't miss the chance to stand by John Wesley's grave, to remember his witness and the faith that shaped the Methodist movement, a faith that likely has shaped you.

Appendix:
Giving Wesley the Final Word

It seemed appropriate for John Wesley to have the final word in this little book. What follows is an excerpt of a tract Wesley first published in 1739 entitled "The Character of a Methodist." I quote it from the final edition of Wesley's tract, A Plain Account of Christian Perfection, *published in 1777.*[1]

"A Methodist is one who loves the Lord his God with all his heart, with all his soul, with all his mind, and with all his strength. God is the joy of his heart, and the desire of his soul, which is continually crying, 'Whom have I in heaven but thee? and there is none upon earth whom I desire besides thee.' My God and my all! 'Thou art the strength of my heart, and my portion for ever.' He is therefore happy in God; yea, always happy, as having in him a well of water springing up unto everlasting life, and over-flowing his soul with peace and joy. Perfect love living now cast out fear, he rejoices evermore. Yea, his joy is full, and all his bones cry out, 'Blessed be the God and Father of our Lord Jesus Christ, who, according to his abundant mercy, hath begotten me again unto a living hope of an inheritance incorruptible and undefiled, reserved in heaven for me.'

"And he, who hath this hope, thus full of immortality, in everything giveth thanks, as knowing this (whatsoever it is) is the will of God in Christ Jesus concerning him. From him therefore he cheerfully receives all, saying, 'Good is the will of the Lord;' and whether he giveth or taketh away, equally blessing the name of the Lord. Whether in ease or pain, whether in sickness or health, whether in life or death, he giveth thanks from the ground of the heart to Him who orders it for good; into whose hands he hath wholly committed his body and soul, 'as into the hands of a faithful Creator.' He is therefore anxiously 'careful for nothing,' as having 'cast all his care on Him that careth for him;' and 'in all things' resting on him, after 'making' his 'request known to him with thanksgiving.'

"For indeed he 'prays without ceasing;' at all times the language of his heart is this, 'Unto thee is my mouth, though without a voice; and my silence speaketh unto thee.' His heart is lifted up to God at all times, and in all places. In this he is never hindered, much less interrupted, by any person or thing. In retirement or company, in leisure, business, or conversation, his heart is ever with the Lord. Whether he lie down, or rise up, 'God is in all his thoughts:' He walks with God continually; having the loving eye of his soul fixed on him, and everywhere 'seeing Him that is invisible.'

"And loving God, he 'loves his neighbor as himself;' he loves every man as his own soul. He loves his enemies, yea, and the enemies of God. And if it be not in his power to 'do good to them that hate' him, yet he ceases not to 'pray for them,' though they spurn his love, and still 'despitefully use him, and persecute him.'

"For he is 'pure in heart.' Love has purified his heart from envy, malice, wrath, and every unkind temper. It has cleansed him from pride, whereof 'only cometh contention;' and he hath now 'put on bowels of mercies, kindness, humbleness of mind, meekness, long-suffering.'

And indeed all possible ground for contention, on his part, is cut off. For none can take from him what he desires, seeing he 'loves not the world, nor any of the things of the world;' but 'all his desire is unto God, and to the remembrance of his name.'

"Agreeable to this his one desire, is this one design of his life; namely, 'to do, not his own will, but the will of Him that sent him.' His one intention at all times and in all places is, not to please himself, but Him whom his soul loveth. He hath a single eye; and because his 'eye is single, his whole body is full of light. The whole is light, as when the bright shining of a candle doth enlighten the house.' God reigns alone; all that is in the soul is 'holiness to the Lord.' There is not a motion in his heart but is according to his will. Every thought that arises points to him, and is in 'obedience to the law of Christ.'

"And the tree is known by its fruits. For, as he loves God, so he 'keeps his commandments;' not only some, or most of them, but all, from the least to the greatest. He is not content to 'keep the whole law and offend in one point,' but has in all points 'a conscience void of offence towards God, and towards man.' Whatever God has forbidden, he avoids; whatever God has enjoined, he does. 'He runs the way of God's commandments,' now He hath set his heart at liberty. It is his glory and joy so to do; it is his daily crown of rejoicing, to 'do the will of God on earth, as it is done in heaven.'

"All the commandments of God he accordingly keeps, and that with all his might; for his obedience is in proportion to his love, the source from whence it flows. And therefore, loving God with all his heart, he serves him with all his strength; he continually presents his soul and 'body a living sacrifice, holy, acceptable to God;' entirely and without reserve devoting himself, all he has, all he is, to his glory. All the talents he has, he constantly employs according to his Master's will; every power and faculty of his soul, every member of his body.

"By consequence, 'whatsoever he doeth, it is all to the glory of God.' In all his employments of every kind, he not only aims at this, which is implied in having a single eye, but actually attains it; his business and his refreshments, as well as his prayers, all serve to this great end. Whether he 'sit in the house, or walk by the way,' whether he lie down, or rise up, he is promoting, in all he speaks or does, the one business of his life. Whether he put on his apparel, or labor, or eat and drink, or divert himself from too wasting labor, it all tends to advance the glory of God, by peace and good-will among men. His one invariable rule is this: 'Whatsoever ye do, in word or deed, do it all in the name of the Lord Jesus, giving thanks to God, even the Father, through him.'

"Nor do the customs of the world at all hinder his 'running the race which is set before him.' He cannot therefore 'lay up treasures upon earth,' no more than he can take fire into his bosom. He cannot speak evil of his neighbor, any more than he can lie either for God or man. He cannot utter an unkind word of any one; for love keeps the door of his lips. He cannot 'speak idle words; no corrupt conversation' ever 'comes out of his mouth;' as is all that is not 'good to the use of edifying,' not fit to 'minister grace to the hearers.' But 'whatsoever things are pure, whatsoever things are lovely, whatsoever things are' justly 'of good report,' he thinks, speaks, and acts, 'adorning the doctrine of God our Savior in all things.'"

May we cultivate the character of this kind of Methodist in our own lives and churches today, and as we do, we will find our hearts revived, our churches renewed, and our communities transformed.

For Further Reading

Kenneth J. Collins, *A Real Christian: The Life of John Wesley*. Nashville: Abingdon, 1999.

> A brief, solid biography that focuses on Wesley himself. While exploring Wesley's ancestry, birth, death, and every major biographical and theological event between, Collins also explores the theme of John Wesley's spiritual growth and maturation.

Kenneth J. Collins and Kason E. Vickers, *The Sermons of John Wesley: A Collection for the Christian Journey*, Nashville: Abingdon Press, 2013.

> This collection of sixty sermons presents each sermon using the text from the Bicentennial Edition of Wesley's works along with a brief introduction and an outline.

Richard P. Heitzenrater, *Wesley and the People Called Methodists* (2nd Edition). Nashville: Abingdon, 2013.

> This second edition of Richard P. Heitzenrater's groundbreaking survey of the Wesleyan movement is the story of the many people who contributed to the theology, organization, and mission of Methodism.

Kenneth Kinghorn, *John Wesley on Christian Beliefs. The Standard Sermons in Modern English, Volume 1: 1-20.* Nashville: Abingdon Press, 2013.

Kenneth Kinghorn, *John Wesley on the Sermon on the Mount. The Standard Sermons in Modern English, Volume 2: 21-33.* Nashville: Abingdon Press, 2013.

Kenneth Kinghorn, *John Wesley on Christian Practice. The Standard Sermons in Modern English, Volume 3: 34-53.* Nashville: Abingdon Press, 2013.

> If the original language is an obstacle to reading Wesley's eighteenth-century sermons, these volumes may help. The author carefully translated Wesley's sermons into comtemporary English while retaining the meaning and nuance.

John Pudney, *John Wesley and His World.* New York: Scribners, 1978.

> This book is out of print but may still be found in libraries or for purchase used. It was recommended to me by Bishop Scott Jones and was helpful in providing photographs of places that were important in Wesley's life.

Alice Russie (ed.), *The Essential Works of John Wesley*. Uhrichsville, Ohio: Barbour Publishing, 2013.

> Russie has pulled together a helpful collection of Wesley's writings from his journals, sermons, and other sources.

Don Thorsen, *Wesley vs. Calvin: Bringing Belief in Line with Practice*. Nashville: Abingdon Press, 2013

> This recent book outlines the significant differences between the theology of John Wesley and John Calvin. Seeing the differences more clearly increases our understanding of Wesley.

Stephen Tomkins, *John Wesley: A Biography*. Grand Rapids: Eerdmans, 2003.

> A compelling portrait of the father of Methodism, written with verve and grounded in thorough research. Tomkins chronicles Wesley's family background and early childhood, his school and university career, and his adult life as a religious leader in England, including a number of key issues in Wesley's increasingly rich religious views.

Henry D. Rack, *Reasonable Enthusiast: John Wesley and the Rise of Methodism, 3rd Edition*. London: Epworth Press, 1989.

> This hefty and well-researched biography presents Wesley in his historical context and corrects some of the common misconceptions about the development of Methodism.

Russell E. Richey, Jeanne Miller Schmidt, and Kenneth E. Rowe, *American Methodism: A Compact History*. Nashville: Abingdon Press, 2012.

> The authors highlight key themes and events in Methodist history in America.

The Wesley Center Online (http://wesley.nnu.edu)

> The Wesley Center Online website is a collection of historical and scholarly resources about the Wesleyan tradition, theology, Christianity, and the Church of the Nazarene.

The Works of John Wesley. Nashville: Abingdon, 1984– .

> This Bicentennial Edition of *The Works of John Wesley*, an ongoing series published by Abingdon Press, is the authoritative print source for Wesley's works.

Notes

Chapter 1

1. "Come, Thou Fount of Every Blessing," *The United Methodist Hymnal*, (Nashville: The United Methodist Publishing House, 1989), no. 400.

2. There is some disagreement as to how many children Samuel and Susanna had, and whether John was the thirteenth, fourteenth, or fifteenth child.

3. Susanna Wesley, letter to Samuel Wesley, February 25, 1712. From John Wesley, *The Works of the Rev. John Wesley*, vol.1. (Philadelphia: D. & S. Neall and W. S. Stockton, 1826), 42.

4. John Wesley journal entry for July 30, 1742. From *The Works of John Wesley*, vol. 19, ed. W. Reginald Ward and Richard P. Heitzenrater (Nashville: Abingdon Press, 1990), 283.

5. John Wesley, *Explanatory Notes upon the New Testament*, Preface (1754), para. 9.

6. John Wesley, Sermon 39, "Catholic Spirit," para. 4. From *The Works of John Wesley*, vol. 2, ed. Albert C Outler. (Nashville: Abingdon Press, 1985), 82.

7. See *Susanna Wesley: The Complete Writings*, ed. Charles Wallace Jr. (Oxford: Oxford University Press, 1997).

8. Winston Churchill, speech at Harrow School, October 29, 1941 (http://www.winstonchurchill.org/learn/speeches/speeches-of -winston-churchill/103-never-give-in).

Chapter 2

1. John Wesley journal entry for May 24, 1738. *The Works of John Wesley*, vol. 18, ed. W. Reginald Ward and Richard P. Heitzenrater (Nashville: Abingdon Press, 1988), 243.

2. Kenneth J. Collins, *A Real Christian: The Life of John Wesley* (Nashville: Abingdon Press, 1999), 19.

3. John Telford, *The Life of John Wesley* (London: Wesleyan Methodist Book Room, 1899), 33, quoted in Collins, *A Real Christian*, 19–20.

4. John Wesley, *A Plain Account of Christian Perfection*, ed. Thomas O. Simmons (Nashville: Publishing House of the Methodist Episcopal Church, South, 1910), 14–20.

5. Jeremy Taylor, *The Rule and Exercises of Holy Living* (1650), chap. 1, section 2.

6. John Wesley, Sermon 26, "Upon our Lord's Sermon on the Mount," para. 2, Discourse 6: "But take heed that ye do not the least thing with a view to your own glory. . . ." From *The Works of John Wesley*, vol. 1, ed. Albert C Outler. (Nashville: Abingdon Press, 1984), 574.

7. John Wesley, *A Plain Account of Christian Perfection*, Simmons, 14–20.

8. Ibid., para. 3.

9. Ibid., para. 4.

10. John Wesley, Sermon 2, "The Almost Christian." From *The Works of John Wesley*, vol. 1, Outler, 140–41.

11. John Wesley, "A Short History of the People Called Methodists" (1781), para. 9.

12. See Henry D. Rack, *Reasonable Enthusiast: John Wesley and the Rise of Methodism* (London: Epworth Press, 1989).

13. See Wesley's letter to Richard Morgan dated October 18, 1732, which describes the beginnings of the Holy Club in 1730.

Chapter 3

1. This phrase is used of Paul's opponents in Acts 21:20, but see Acts 22:3-4; Galatians 1:14.

2. Martin Luther's Exposition on Psalm 45. *Luther's Works*, vol. 12: Selected Psalms 1, eds. J. J. Pelikan, H. C. Oswald, and H. T. Lehmann (St. Louis: Concordia Publishing House, 1955), 273.

3. *What Luther Says: An Anthology*, ed. Ewald M. Plass (St. Louis: Concordia Publishing House, 1959), 3:1226.

4. John Wesley, letter to Mrs. Pendarves, July 19, 1731, as quoted in Collins, *A Real Christian*, 33.

5. Richard P. Heitzenrater, *Wesley and the People Called Methodists*, 2nd ed. (Nashville: Abingdon, 2013), 64, citing journal entry in Wesley, *The Works of John Wesley*, vol. 18, Ward and Heitzenrater, 222.

6. John Wesley journal entry for October 14, 1735. *The Works of John Wesley*, vol. 18, Ward and Heitzenrater, 136–37.

7. John Wesley journal entry for January 25, 1736. *The Works of John Wesley*, vol. 18, Ward and Heitzenrater, 143.

8. Wesley eschewed hard liquor, though he drank small amounts of wine and beer, which he believed were medicinal in moderation. Methodists taught temperance, not complete abstinence from alcohol, but they had seen the impact of hard liquor and generally were taught to avoid it. (Wesley's mother, Susanna, believed clergy should abstain.) In 1864, the Methodist Episcopal Church in

America called upon its churches to use only unfermented grape juice for Holy Communion. Five years later a Methodist pastor and dentist developed a process to pasteurize grape juice to stop it from fermenting. His name was Thomas Welch, and most Methodist churches have been using Welch's grape juice for Holy Communion ever since.

9. See Stephen Tomkins, *John Wesley: A Biography* (Grand Rapids: Eerdman's, 2003), 49.

10. See the *Didache* 8:1-3. The *Didache* dates to the late first or early second century.

11. John Wesley journal entry for June 22, 1736. *The Works of John Wesley*, vol. 18, Ward and Heitzenrater, 228.

12. John Wesley journal entry for March 4, 1738. *The Works of John Wesley*, vol. 18, Ward and Heitzenrater, 161–62

13. John Wesley journal entry for May 24, 1738. *The Works of John Wesley*, vol. 18, Ward and Heitzenrater, 249–50.

14. Paul Tillich, *The Shaking of the Foundations* (New York: Scribners, 1948), chap. 19.

Chapter 4

1. John Wesley, Sermon 45, "The New Birth," *The Works of John Wesley*, vol. 2, Outler, 193–94.

2. As many as 500,000 Africans were enslaved and carried to America on ships sailing out of Bristol.

3. John Wesley journal entry for March 29 and April 2, 1739. *The Works of John Wesley*, vol. 19, Ward and Heitzenrater, 46.

4. John Wesley journal entry for April 8, 1739. *The Works of John Wesley*, vol. 19, Ward and Heitzenrater, 48.

5. Heitzenrater, *Wesley and the People Called Methodists*, 2nd ed., 110.

6. It should be noted that Wesley did not see this as a church. He was a priest in the Church of England, and this was a meeting house or preaching house.

7. John Wesley, "Rules of the Band Societies" (December 25, 1738), point 4. The dating of these guidelines is 1738, before Wesley came to Bristol, but Richard Heitzenrater suggests the date is 1739, after the building of New Room at Bristol. See Heitzenrater, *Wesley and the People Called Methodists*, 2nd ed., 99.

8. George Whitefield and those who followed him were an exception. They were Calvinistic Methodists, or Methodist Calvinists.

9. J. B. Wakeley, *Anecdotes of the Wesleys: Illustrative of Their Character and Personal History* (New York: Carlton and Lanahan, 1870), 114–15.

Chapter 5

1. Heitzenrater, *Wesley and the People Called Methodists*, 2nd ed., 47.

2. See John Wesley, "A Short History of the People Called Methodists" (1781), para. 9.

Chapter 6

1. John Wesley, Sermon 4, "Scriptural Christianity." *The Works of John Wesley*, vol.1, Outler, 179.

2. John Wesley journal entry for August 28, 1748. *The Works of John Wesley*, vol. 20, ed. W. Reginald Ward and Richard P. Heitzenrater (Nashville: Abingdon Press, 1991), 245.

3. King recounted the story in a sermon on January 27, 1957, to his Dexter congregation and quotations were published by the *Montgomery Advertiser;* but the experience actually took place in January 1956.

4. John Wesley journal entry for March 3, 1788. *The Works of John Wesley*, vol. 24, ed. W. Reginald Ward and Richard P. Heitzenrater (Nashville: Abingdon Press, 2003), 70. See also Brycchan Carey, "John Wesley's *Thoughts Upon Slavery* and the Language of the Heart," *The Bulletin of the John Rylands Library*, 85:2-3 (Summer/Autumn 2003), 277.

5. John Wesley, Sermon 50, "The Use of Money, *The Works of John Wesley*, vol. 2, Outler, 268–80.

6. John Wesley's death and his final words are related in an addendum to his published *Journal* and in *Wesley and Early Methodism: An Historical Text-Book*, by Angela K. Davis (New York: Phillips and Hunt, 1884), 114.

7. "I'll Praise My Maker While I've Breath," *The United Methodist Hymnal*, no. 60.

8. "A Covenant Prayer in the Wesleyan Tradition," *The United Methodist Hymnal*, no. 607.

Appendix

1. John Wesley, *A Plain Account of Christian Perfection*. Thomas O. Simmons (ed.). (Nashville: Publishing House of the Methodist Episcopal Church, South, 1910), 14-20.

Image Credits

Photographs courtesy of Adam Hamilton.

Image of Oxford courtesy of ©iStock.com/andrearoad.

Image of Wesley Monument at Fort Pulaski courtesy of Deborah Crane.

Maps by Marcia Myatt.

Acknowledgments

I am profoundly grateful for the people of my congregation, The United Methodist Church of the Resurrection, for allowing me time away to travel to England, meet with scholars, and read in preparation for writing this little book. The Lilly Endowment Clergy Renewal Grant helped fund my travel to England, and Educational Opportunities Tours provided a large portion of the support needed for filming the videos that accompany this study.

I am grateful to my bishop and friend, Scott Jones and his wife Mary Lou, who joined LaVon and me in England with our film crew, Lee Rudeen and Natalie Cleveland. Bishop Jones is a Wesley Scholar, and he and Mary Lou were invaluable resources on our trip.

I am grateful for the help of Dr. Richard Heitzenrater, my seminary professor who taught me most of what I know about John Wesley. He met with me before I embarked on this project. He read the first draft of the book and offered an extremely helpful critique that made the book stronger. Any errors that remain are my own or reflect my interpretation of Wesley.

Dr. Geordan Hammond of the Manchester Wesley Research Centre in Manchester, England, also offered valuable suggestions, as did Professors Hal Knight and Randy Maddox, both outstanding Wesley scholars. They provided feedback and corrections to the manuscript.

This book would not have been written without my publishing team at Abingdon Press: Susan Salley, Ron Kidd, Alan Vermilye, Tim Cobb, Marcia Myatt, Tracey Craddock, Camilla Myers, Sally Sharpe, and Sonia Worsham. Their help in this project was critical.

Special thanks to Jill Reddig, who took my sermon manuscripts and from them crafted the first draft of the book.

Finally, I'd like to thank my wife, LaVon, who has been my partner, friend, collaborator, and companion not only during the writing of this book but in the journey we began thirty-one years ago when we joined The United Methodist Church and answered the call to be part of its renewal. Together we've learned from, and been shaped by, the faith of John Wesley.

About the Author

ADAM HAMILTON is senior pastor of The United Methodist Church of the Resurrection in Leawood, Kansas, one of the fastest growing, most highly visible churches in the country. *The Church Report* named Hamilton's congregation the most influential mainline church in America and PBS's Religion and Ethics Newsweekly identified him as one of the "Ten People to Watch." In 2013, Adam was invited to deliver the sermon at the National Prayer Service in Washington's National Cathedral as part of the presidential inauguration festivities. A master at explaining questions of faith in a down-to earth fashion, he is the author of many books including *The Journey*, *The Way*, *24 Hours That Changed the World*, *Enough*, *Why: Making Sense of God's Will*, *When Christians Get it Wrong*, *Seeing Gray in a World of Black and White*, *Forgiveness*, *Love to Stay*, and *Making Sense of the Bible*.

Educational Opportunities Tours

I would like to thank Educational Opportunities Tours (EO) for their support of the work and travel that made this book possible.

Educational Opportunities has now worked closely with me for more than fifteen years, beginning with my first journey to the Holy Land and continuing with this most recent trip through the British Isles to follow in the footsteps of John Wesley. Their advice and support have helped us invite you, the reader, along for these journeys, following the life of Wesley, walking the road to Bethlehem, and seeing the sites of Jesus' last hours. EO will provide valuable advice and counsel when my team and I next travel to Italy, Turkey, and Greece to trace the ministry of the Apostle Paul.

–Adam Hamilton

For more information, go to www.eo.TravelWithUs.com.

Not a Silent Night

Prepare your heart for Christmas by looking at Jesus' life through Mary's eyes, starting from the end of her own life, through the life of her son, and back finally to that night in Bethlehem.

Along the way, discover the hope of resurrection found in the garden, the salvation gift of the cross, the promise of a new way to live, and the ever-present gift of God's grace.

As Mary learned, God doesn't promise a perfect, peaceful life or a silent, holy night. Sometimes it's hard and painful and scary. Yet, in the messiness of life, God is at work, bringing blessing out of pain. That's the message of Christmas.

ISBN 978-1-4267-7184-2

DVD and small group leader guide also available.

Revival

Wesley's message and his faith continue to speak to 21st-century Christians—calling for a revival of our hearts and souls so that our world might be changed.

Join Adam Hamilton for a six-week journey as he travels to England, following the life of John Wesley and exploring his defining characteristics of a Wesleyan Christian. Wesley's story is our story. It strengthens our faith and challenges us to rediscover our spiritual passion.

Read *Revival* on your own or, for a more in-depth study, enjoy it with a small group.

ISBN 978-1-4267-7884-1

Abingdon Press™

Study Resources

This six-session DVD features Adam Hamilton guiding us through a six-week Bible study tracing the life of John Wesley throughout England. Perfect for adult and youth classes, this study will deepen people's faith by calling them to a devout and holy life while defining what the Christian life looks like through the eyes of a Wesleyan Christian. All video sessions are closed captioned and run approximately 10-15 minutes each.

ISBN 978-1-4267-7682-3

A small group leader guide and study resources for children and youth are also available.

The Way

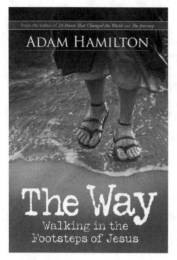

Travel to the Holy Land in this third volume of Adam Hamilton's Bible study trilogy on the life of Jesus. Once again, Hamilton approaches his subject matter with thoughtfulness and wisdom as he did with Jesus' crucifixion in *24 Hours That Changed the World* and with Jesus' birth in *The Journey*. Using historical background, archaeological findings, and stories of the faith, Hamilton retraces the footsteps of Jesus from his baptism to the temptations to the heart of his ministry, including the people he loved, the enemies he made, the parables he taught, and the roads that he traveled.

Read *The Way* on your own or, for a more in-depth study, enjoy it with a small group.

ISBN 978-1-4267-5251-3

Continue the Way

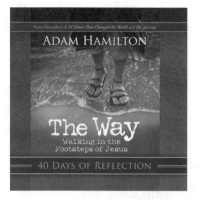

This companion volume to *The Way* functions beautifully on its own or as part of the churchwide experience. Adam Hamilton offers daily devotions that enable us to pause, meditate, and emerge changed forever. Ideal for use during Lent, the reflections include Scripture, stories from Hamilton's own ministry, and prayers.

ISBN 978-1-4267-5252-0

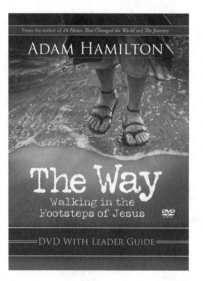

Join Adam Hamilton in the Holy Land as he retraces the life and ministry of Jesus Christ in this DVD study. Perfect for adult and youth classes, the DVD includes a Leader Guide to facilitate small group discussion about the book, the devotions, and the DVD. Each session averages ten minutes.

ISBN 978-1-4267-5253-7

Study resources for children and youth are also available.

Abingdon Press™

The Journey

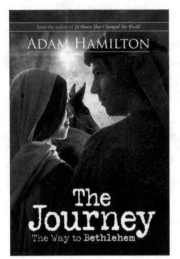

Journey with Adam Hamilton as he travels from Nazareth to Bethlehem in this fascinating look at the birth of Jesus Christ. As he did with Jesus' crucifixion in *24 Hours That Changed the World*, Hamilton once again approaches a world-changing event with thoughtfulness. Using historical information, archaeological data, and a personal look at some of the stories surrounding the birth, the most amazing moment in history will become more real and heartfelt as you walk along this road.

Read *The Journey* on your own or, for a more in-depth study, enjoy it with a small group.

ISBN 978-1-4267-1425-2

Continue the Journey

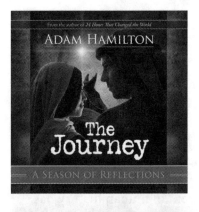

Go deeper on your Christmas journey with *A Season of Reflection*. With Scripture, stories, and prayer, this collection of 28 daily readings brings the well-known story into your daily spiritual life.

ISBN 978-1-4267-1426-9

Join Adam Hamilton as he travels the roads to Bethlehem in this video journey. In five video segments, Adam explores Bethlehem, the routes the Holy Family traveled, the traditional site of the stable in Bethlehem, the ruins of Herodium, and more.

ISBN 978-1-4267-1999-8

Study resources for children and youth and
an app for families are also available.
Learn more at JourneyThisChristmas.com

24 Hours That Changed the World

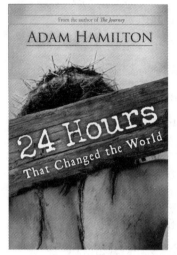

Walk with Jesus on his final day. Sit beside him at the Last Supper. Pray with him in Gethsemane. Follow him to the cross. Desert him. Deny him. Experience the Resurrection.

No single event in human history has received more attention than the suffering and crucifixion of Jesus of Nazareth. In this heartbreaking, inspiring book, Adam Hamilton guides us, step by step, through the last 24 hours of Jesus' life.

ISBN 978-0-687-46555-2

"Adam Hamilton combines biblical story, historical detail, theological analysis, spiritual insight, and pastoral warmth to retell the narrative of Jesus' last and greatest hours."
—**Leith Anderson,** author of *The Jesus Revolution*

Devotions and Study Resources

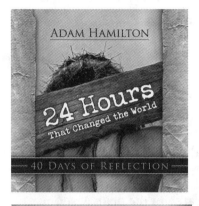

For the Lent and Easter season, Adam Hamilton offers 40 days of devotions enabling us to pause, reflect, dig deeper, and emerge from the experience changed forever.

ISBN 978-1-4267-0031-6

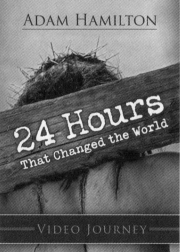

Travel with Adam through this companion DVD visiting the sites, walking where Jesus walked along the road that led to the pain and triumph of the cross.

The DVD includes seven sessions plus an introduction and bonus clips. Each session averages ten minutes.

ISBN 978-0-687-65970-8

Also available:
Older and Younger Children's study sessions
and youth small group resources

Love to Stay

Falling in love is easy, but staying in love takes courage, hard work, and lots of grace. In his compelling, conversational style, Adam Hamilton explores the ups, downs, and how-to's of marriage, and how, with God's help, we can make love last.

Hamilton draws on an extensive survey of thousands of couples and singles, the latest research in the field, wisdom from the Bible, and stories from his own ministry and marriage to explore what it takes to create and sustain healthy, meaningful romantic relationships across the course of a lifetime.

ISBN 978-1-4267-5951-2

"*Love to Stay* is an intensely researched, biblical, and intensely practical. Adam Hamilton is not just a devoted husband and pastor; he is committed to making marriage a stronger and healthier and deeper relationship."

—**John Ortberg,** Senior Pastor of Menlo Park Presbyterian Church and author of *Who Is This Man?*

—**Nancy Ortberg,** author of *Looking for God*

AVAILABLE WHEREVER FINE BOOKS ARE SOLD.
FOR MORE INFORMATION ABOUT ADAM HAMILTON, VISIT WWW.ADAMHAMILTON.ORG

Forgiveness

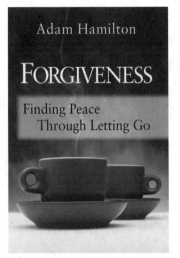

Adam Hamilton equates our need to forgive with carrying a backpack filled with rocks. Over time the tiny pepples and giant boulders weigh us down and break more than our spirit. In *Forgiveness: Finding Peace Through Letting Go*, Hamilton shows readers how to receive the freedom that comes with forgiving—even if the person needing forgiveness is ourselves.

Read *Forgiveness* on your own or, for a more in-depth study, enjoy it with a small group

ISBN 978-1-4267-4044-2

"Adam Hamilton not only reminds us about the importance of reconnecting the broken pieces of our lives, but shows how the process of grace and forgiveness is possibly our most complete picture of God."
—**Shane Stanford,** author of *Making Life Matter: Embracing the Joy in the Everyday*

Why?

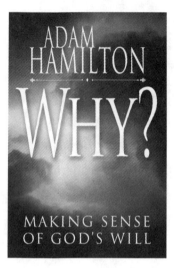

When the ground shakes, and a poor nation's economy is destroyed; when the waters rise, washing away a community's hopes and dreams; when a child suffers neglect and abuse; when violence tears apart nations: Where is God?

In *Why? Making Sense of God's Will*, best-selling author Adam Hamilton brings fresh insight to the age-old question of how to understand the will of God. Rejecting simplistic answers and unexamined assumptions, Hamilton addresses how we can comprehend God's plan for the world and ourselves.

ISBN 978-1-4267-1478-8

"I recommend this book to anyone who longs to leave behind simplistic answers and discover a God who invites them into a collaborative process of bringing redemption, love, and hope to a world in desperate need."
—**Lynne Hybels,** author of *Nice Girls Don't Change the World*